EXPLORING SCIENCE

LEVEL

4 ALL AROUND US

EXPLORING SCIENCE 4
ALL AROUND US

REVIEWERS

Dr. Jill Sible: Professor of Biological Sciences, Virginia Tech, Blacksburg, VA

Dr. Giti Khodaparast: Associate Professor of Physics, Virginia Tech, Blacksburg, VA

Katie Rexrode: Science Coach, VISTA (Virginia Initiative for Science Teaching and Achievement) through Virginia Commonwealth University, Richmond, VA and former third grade teacher, Hanover County Public Schools.

Wendy Just: 4th grade teacher, Kersey Creek Elementary School, Mechanicsville, VA

ADDITIONAL CONTRIBUTORS

Dr. Brenda Brand: Associate Professor, Department of Teaching and Learning, Virginia Tech, Blacksburg, VA

Dr. Joseph Formaggio: Associate Professor of Physics, Massachusetts Institute of Technology, Cambridge, MA ("Force, Motion and Energy" and "Electricity and Magnetism" sections)

Jessica Garrett: K-12 Education Outreach, Edgerton Center, Massachusetts Institute of Technology, Cambridge, MA

Ben Ligon: 6th grade math and science teacher, Belmont Public School, Belmont, MA

Dr. Melissa Matusevich: Former supervisor of Social Studies and Library Media, Montgomery County, VA, Public Schools

Dr. Donald Zeigler: Professor of Geography and Political Science, Old Dominion University, Norfolk, VA

TEACHER MATERIALS

Bree Linton, Richmond, VA • **Katie Rexrode**, Beaverdam, VA
Reviewed by:
Leslie Swenson, Henrico, VA • **Lara Samuels**, Richmond, VA
Megan Ellington, Hanover, VA • **Wendy Just**, Hanover, VA
Assessments:
Lisa Arnold, Richmond, VA

ISBN 978-1-935813-22-4   Printed in the USA

GO AHEAD! TAKE A GOOD LOOK!

Everything you do involves science. Got goose bumps at a scary movie? Science! Baking a tray of gooey brownies? Science! Doing a cool wheelie on your skateboard—and sometimes falling flat on your face? Most definitely science!

EVERY DAY IS AN EXPERIMENT

Each and every day brings you a chance to learn more about the world around you—to explore unseen worlds and discover how the universe works. Science is an awesome adventure.

The knowledge you gain this year could set you on the road to a thrilling future. Perhaps you will become an undersea explorer, a moon-walking astronaut, or a world-famous inventor. Perhaps you will devote your life to saving other lives. Maybe one day you will discover how to turn the sun's rays into a safe and inexpensive fuel.

How do you get started? Science begins with your eyes and ears and springs to life with that marvelous three-pound organ—your brain.

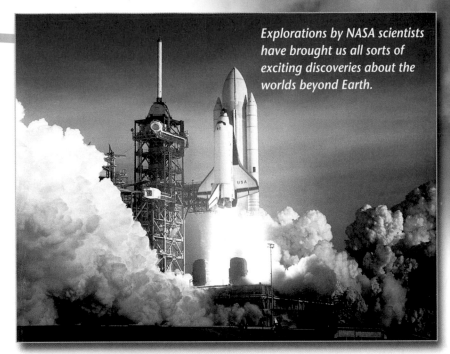

Explorations by NASA scientists have brought us all sorts of exciting discoveries about the worlds beyond Earth.

TWISTER!
Find out how one of nature's most destructive forces gets its start in a fluffy little cloud.

WHAT ADVENTURES AWAIT?

Spend some time with crash-test dummies and learn how roller coasters save and spend energy. Go nose to nose with a pollen-packing bee and a smelly, stink-squirting skunk. Blast off to Mars, and explore the inside of a category four hurricane.

There are planets to explore in outer space, but there are also wonderful treasures right here in Virginia. Explore the beautiful Chesapeake Bay watershed and the ancient peaks of the Appalachian range. Meet furry animals, dig up precious minerals, and dive along the Atlantic coast.

You may not be an astronaut or a meteorologist yet—but you are already a scientist! Just keep looking, listening, and asking lots of questions.

FROM TOO-SMALL-TO-SEE TO AS-BIG-AS-THE-SUN

Some of this year's discoveries will be tiny—no bigger than a seed the size of this period. Others will be electrifying. They might even make your hair stand straight up! Some explorations will make you a better caretaker of our planet. Others might even make you laugh.

So grab your safety glasses and bring your imagination. You will definitely be needing it. Science *is* all around you. And all you have to do is take a good look around you and ask yourself,

"I WONDER WHY..."

SAFETY FIRST!

Science is exciting and lots of fun, but only if you follow these ten important rules.

WHAT MATTERS MOST?

It cannot be said often enough. Safety is the most important part of science. Some science experiments take place in the classroom, others will take place in your home or out in nature. Each type of experiment calls for these important safety-smarts.

1. PROTECT YOUR EYES

When working with liquids, or experimenting with batteries, circuits, and electricity, always wear safety glasses. It is easy to splash something into an eye. Even water can hurt!

2. TELL A GROWN-UP

Always tell your teacher, a parent, or other grown-up that you are going to be working on an experiment.

3. STAY SAFE OUTDOORS

Watch out for poison ivy, insects, and the occasional snake. Wear long pants tucked into your socks when working in fields with tall grass to keep ticks from biting. Tell a grown-up where you are going.

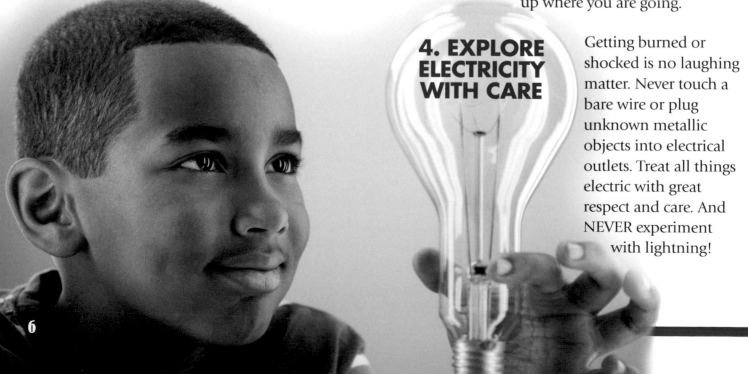

4. EXPLORE ELECTRICITY WITH CARE

Getting burned or shocked is no laughing matter. Never touch a bare wire or plug unknown metallic objects into electrical outlets. Treat all things electric with great respect and care. And NEVER experiment with lightning!

5. DON'T DRINK FROM THE LAB WARE

Beakers and flasks are for chemicals, not milk or juice. Chemical leftovers can remain in lab ware even if it has been washed.

6. RESPECT THE SUN'S POWER

Use sunscreen! Wear sunglasses! When you are experimenting outdoors, don't end up fried to a crisp. Never, ever look directly at the sun.

7. WASH YOUR HANDS

When you are done with your experiments, wash your hands. If you are working with chemicals, always wear protective gloves and safety glasses.

REMEMBER THESE IMPORTANT SAFETY TIPS

All it takes is one careless mistake for something to go wrong. If you follow these guidelines, you and your classmates will be safe.

8. HOT AND COLD CALL FOR CARE

When experimenting with ice or steam, be extra careful. Frigid temperatures can damage your skin. Steam can lead to very painful burns.

9. ASK FIRST, TASTE SECOND

Sweet? Sour? Bitter? Sometimes an experiment might call for you to use your sense of taste. Always ask your teacher or a grown-up first before tasting something.

10. HANDLE GLASS WITH CARE

Some lab ware is made of glass and will shatter if dropped or smacked against a hard surface like a desk. Glass equipment calls for extra care.

CHAPTER 1

SCIENTIFIC INVESTIGATION

What do all good experiments have in common?

How do you share your findings?

What is the scientific method?

THE SECRETS OF SMART SCIENTISTS

Science starts with lots of questions.
Here's how scientists find the answers.

MYSTERIOUS WORLD

A scientist and a detective have a lot in common. They are both trying to solve a mystery. To do this they must gather clues. They need to carefully observe. They must record every detail they see. They will have hunches and "suspects." In the end they may be able to solve the mystery. Case closed!

What about the world puzzles you? Do you love sports? Think about the difference between a soccer ball and a baseball. Do you like to bake? Why does cake batter rise? Are you a penguin lover? Surviving the brutal Antarctic cold seems almost impossible. How do penguins do it? The world is full of mysteries!

SENSES AND SCIENCE

You have five spectacular senses. Use them! As you watch the clouds roll by, smell a rose, eat an ice cream cone, pat a kitten, or listen to a twangy electric guitar, write down any thoughts or questions you might have. Then, follow this series of steps to try to solve your particular mystery. These steps are called the **scientific method**.

THE SCIENTIFIC METHOD

- **Make an observation and ask a question.**
What? Where? How? When? Why? Start the process with one of these words.

- **Do some background research.**
Go to the library, visit a science museum, or explore an educational website. Gain a better understanding of your subject.

- **Construct a hypothesis.**
Think of a possible answer to your question. A hypothesis is an educated guess based on what you already know. It must be "testable."

- **Design an experiment to test your hypothesis.**
This should prove whether or not your hypothesis is correct. But even a "wrong" answer is helpful in the scientific process. Repeat your experiments.

- **Collect and analyze your data.**
Write down your data. Draw or take photos of your observations. Think about what your data tell you.

- **Develop a conclusion and share your findings.**
Use charts and graphs to share data with peers. Determine whether or not your hypothesis was correct. State what you learned and think of new questions.

- **Cite your research.**
If you have used any books, magazines, or the Internet, share your sources.

OBSERVATION

Write down *only* what your senses see, hear, smell, feel, or taste. Don't let guesses or past experience cloud your thoughts. Be sure to write down all the details.

"I saw three baby sparrows in a nest in the oak tree. I heard them chirping loudly at 3:47 P.M."

INFERENCE

If people are bundled up in mufflers and fleecy hats, you might **infer** that it is cold out. An **inference** is a conclusion based on the best data you have at the moment, but those bundled up people might be actors in a play. Don't let your eyes fool the rest of your senses!

"I observed Princess circling her bowl and barking. I inferred that she was thirsty."

HYPOTHESIS /PREDICTION

Remember these two words: **IF** and **THEN**. A **hypothesis** is a statement that begins with an IF, such as "IF I place these plants in a dark room, THEN they will not grow." A hypothesis is a testable prediction based on scientific reasoning. Based on what you learn from your research, you can make an educated guess about the outcome of an event: "I know that baby birds need food, so I **predict** the mother bird will bring some." You can predict what *should* happen based on scientific principles.

"If I leave the baking powder out of grandma's cake recipe, then the cake will not rise properly."

EXPERIMENT

This is the time to put your hypothesis to the test. Your **experiment** is the most important part of the scientific method. Make sure you only test one hypothesis at a time. Keep careful notes and record all your data. Repeat the experiment at least three times to make sure your results were not an accident.

"My experiment will test how plant growth is affected by different colors of lightbulb."

CONCLUSION

Was your prediction correct? Did your hypothesis prove true? By carefully following the scientific method, you should be able to come up with an answer to your original question. Sometimes an experiment does not answer a question, so you'll just have to keep trying!

"The combination of direct sun and 1/2 cup of water every three days resulted in the largest flowers."

THE BEST TOOLS

You would never try to hammer a nail with a ball of cotton. You need the right tools to do a good job. Scientists depend on these items.

MEASURING UP

In two separate labs—one in Bejing, China, and the other in Fairfax, Virginia—a group of scientists are working together to create a new way to protect plants from hungry insects. How can they share their discoveries?

Many years ago it was decided that science needed a "common language of measurement" that would be the same all over the globe. That system is called the **metric system**, a system is based on the number ten.

Science is all about being exact, and most experiments depend on measurements. Scientists use reliable tools to make their measurements. They carefully organize their data, then share their discoveries. They ask "how heavy," "how tall," "how fast," and "how hot." Weight, length, elapsed time, and temperature are all measurements used to reach conclusions.

FROM LITERS TO METERS

The United States is one of only a handful of countries that does not use the metric system in day-to-day life, but America's scientists always use metric units.

We use centimeter rulers and meter sticks to measure length. Scales and balances measure mass in grams. Graduated cylinders and beakers measure milliliters. Celsius thermometers record temperatures.

- **Meters** (*me-terz*) Units of measure for height, length, width, or distance.

- **Kilograms** (*kill-uh-gramz*) Units of measure for mass.

- **Liters** (*lee-terz*) Units of measure for volume.

- **Celsius** (*Sell-see-us*) Units of measure for temperature.

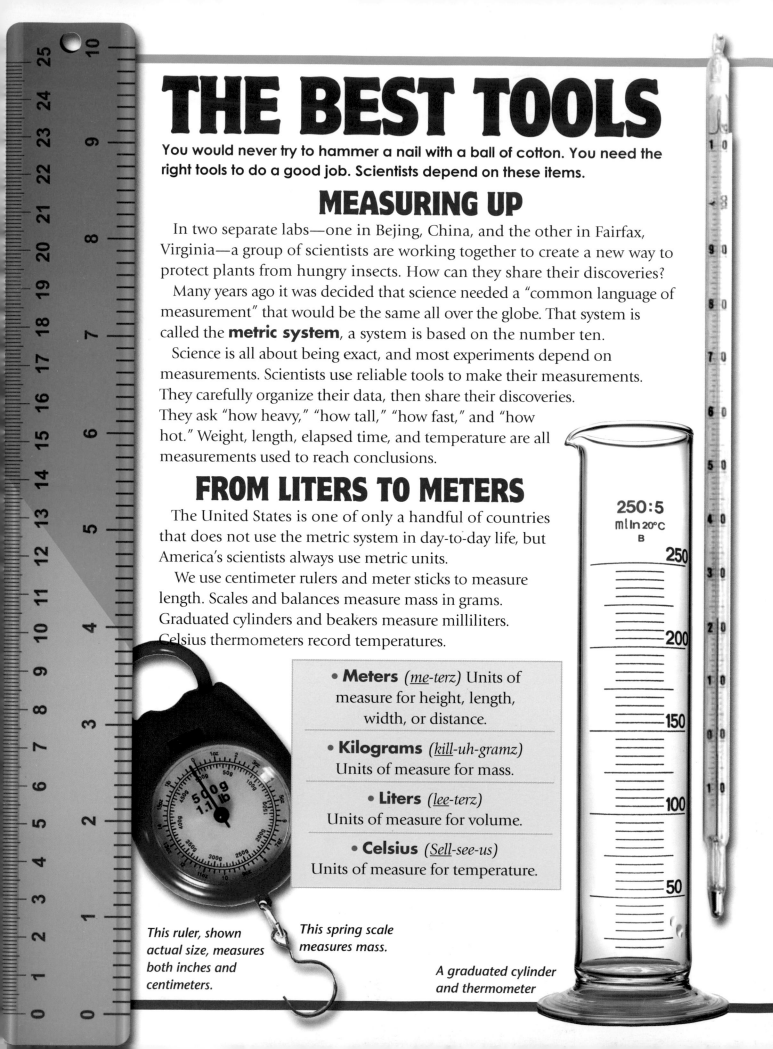

This ruler, shown actual size, measures both inches and centimeters.

This spring scale measures mass.

A graduated cylinder and thermometer

MEASURING AMOUNTS

Sometimes, experiments involve measuring very small or very large amounts. Instead of using complicated fractions, the metric system uses sub-groupings. A prefix—a little mini-word—before each unit of measure tells you how big or small it is.

- **milli** = one-thousandth (¹⁄₁₀₀₀) of something. For example, a milliliter is ¹⁄₁₀₀₀ of a liter.

- **centi** = one-hundredth (¹⁄₁₀₀) of something. A centimeter is ¹⁄₁₀₀ of a meter.

- **kilo** = one thousand of something. This is a bigger measurement. For example, a kilometer is a thousand meters. A kilogram is a thousand grams.

In countries that use the metric system, kilometers instead of miles are used to measure distance. Kilograms instead of pounds are used to measure mass. Soft drinks are sold by the liter, and cough syrup is swallowed by the milliliter. When you know these prefixes, it becomes easy to know whether you are dealing with large or very small measurements.

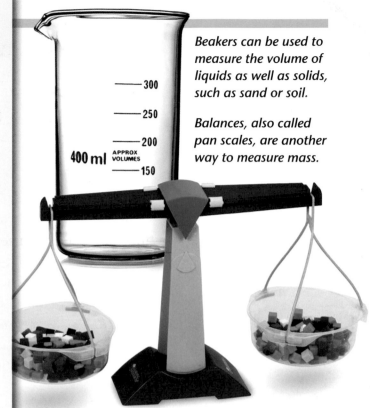

Beakers can be used to measure the volume of liquids as well as solids, such as sand or soil.

Balances, also called pan scales, are another way to measure mass.

HOW HOT OR COLD?

Measuring temperatures in science calls for the use of the Celsius scale (°C). Using this system, water freezes at 0° and boils at 100°. When you compare it to the Fahrenheit scale—the way we measure temperatures in our daily weather reports—with water freezing at 32° and boiling at 212°, the Celsius scale is much simpler.

TOOLS IN THE FIELD
This young scientist is using two types of lab equipment. What measurements do you think he is making?

Remember these abbreviations

- **Millimeters = mm**
- **Centimeters = cm**
- **Meters = m**
- **Kilometers = km**

- **Grams = g**
- **Kilograms = kg**

- **Milliliters = ml**
- **Liters = l**

- **Centigrade = °C**

Below is an example of a well-conducted experiment.

Some experiments begin with a "whoops."

LET THE EXPERIMENTS BEGIN!

After slipping on an icy patch, Ali wondered if certain materials might help ice melt faster. She found out that the highway department spread a mixture of dirt and salt on icy roadways. She knew her next-door-neighbor simply used handfuls of coarse salt on icy front steps. Ali read a magazine article that said that powdered laundry detergent worked well as a melting agent. So Ali set out to conduct an experiment to prove which worked the best.

FROM QUESTION TO EXPERIMENT

Where did Ali begin? When you have a question that needs answering, you must develop a **hypothesis** to explain what may happen, then design an experiment to test that hypothesis. Last year we learned that a hypothesis was a prediction that had to be tested to be proven correct. What was Ali's hypothesis about the ice?

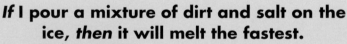

If I pour a mixture of dirt and salt on the ice, then it will melt the fastest.

Ali **inferred** that since her town used a mixture of dirt and salt on the roadways, then it must be the best at melting ice. Since that was what her town used, she **predicted** it would also work best in her experiment. It was time to design her experiment. Ali began by thinking of how to test her hypothesis. She gathered four identical ice cube trays. With a graduated cylinder she poured exactly 30 ml of water into each compartment and placed the trays on the same shelf in the freezer. She waited 24 hours, until the water had completely frozen.

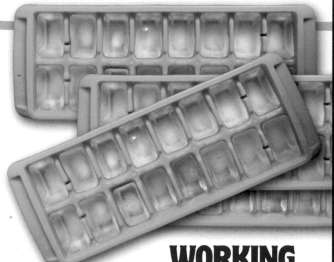

WORKING WITH VARIABLES

Ali's **independent variable** was the type of melting agent used. To make it a fair test, she measured equal amounts of each of her agents and spread each over the identical bowls of ice. Her **dependent variable** was the melting rate of the ice cubes. Which would melt fastest? Ali set a timer, pulled up a chair, watched, and waited.

A good experiment always has **constants**. In Ali's experiment, some of the constants were the size of ice cube and amount of melting agent used. Why are constants important? If Ali had used more or fewer ice cubes, or cubes that were bigger than others, they would not have melted at the same rate. Her experiment would be flawed. If she used different quantities of salt or detergent, her data would also be unbalanced. Her **control** —ice with nothing on it—showed what happens when ice has no melting agents added to it.

DO IT AGAIN

Don't forget! Every experiment should be repeated at least three times!

ALI'S ICY EXPERIMENT

Hypothesis: If I pour a mixture of 100 grams of dirt and 100 grams of salt on 16 ice cubes, then it will melt faster than pouring 200 grams of just salt or 200 grams of detergent on bowls with 16 ice cubes.

Prediction: The dirt/salt mixture will melt the ice faster than the plain salt or the detergent.

Data:

Dirt and salt mixture	Salt only	Detergent only	Control: No melting agent
62 minutes	48 minutes	86 minutes	123 minutes

I conclude that using a melting agent caused ice to melt faster. Using pure salt caused the ice to melt faster than any other melting agent.

I performed the entire experiment three times to insure accuracy. My results were similar every time. Each time, the salt by itself melted the ice the fastest.

Conclusion: Plain salt was the best melting agent.

SHARING YOUR DATA

You have been researching some ideas for experiments.
How will you gather and present your findings?

WITH TOOLS IN HAND

You have been looking around, thinking of lots of questions that you have about the world. You are almost ready to launch an investigation, do an experiment, and share your discoveries with your classmates. One important thing you will have to do is record and share your data.

Keeping careful records, and then presenting your information in a clear and easy-to-understand format, is a must-do.

DESCRIBING MR. BINGLEY

QUALITATIVE:
- LIGHT BROWN AND BEIGE
- SQUISHY
- BLACK EYES
- ARMS AND LEGS THAT MOVE
- COVERED WITH FUR-LIKE FABRIC

QUANTITATIVE:
- OVERALL HEIGHT 30 CM
- WAIST 15 CM
- MASS 0.7 KG

SPEAK LIKE A SCIENTIST

·················

Qualitative
(*kwa-lih-tay-tiv*)

Describing the quality of something by its relative size, the way it looks, or its special properties. This data does not rely on measuring tools.

QUALITATIVE OR QUANTITATIVE DATA: WHICH IS WHICH?

Think about a stuffed teddy bear. There are several ways you can describe it. You might say that it's furry, soft, and brown. These observations are **qualitative** data. You can also say that the stuffed bear is 30 cm tall by 15 cm wide at its tummy, and its mass is 0.7 kg. Those specific measurements are called **quantitative** data. Both kinds of data are very useful when you are doing an experiment or studying rocks, plants, or animals.

SPEAK LIKE A SCIENTIST

·················

Quantitative
(*kwan-tuh-tay-tiv*)

Describing something using number measurements such as weight or height.

USING GRAPHS

After you have finished an investigation, you might have all sorts of numbers and descriptions written in your notebook. What do you do with all your data? How can you share it?

A graph takes numerical or descriptive information and sorts it into a quickly understood, visual format. It communicates your data. There are several different kinds of graphs, but **bar graphs** and **line graphs** are two of the most commonly used.

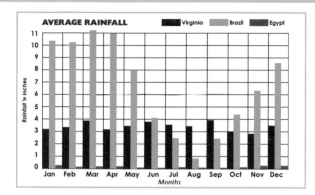

AVERAGE RAINFALL — Virginia, Brazil, Egypt

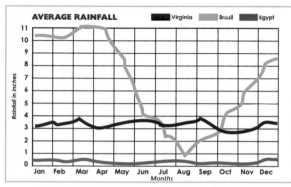

AVERAGE RAINFALL — Virginia, Brazil, Egypt

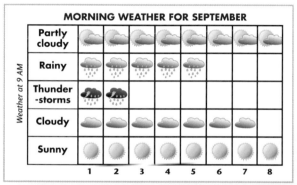

MORNING WEATHER FOR SEPTEMBER

BAR GRAPHS

This kind of graph uses rectangular bars to show quantitative data. Some bar graphs use vertical bars, others use horizontal bars. This graph compares rainfall in Virginia, Brazil, and Egypt. Can you quickly tell where it rains the most? In what month does Virginia have almost the same amount of rain as Brazil?

LINE GRAPHS

Line graphs are often used to show changes over a period of time. This graph shares the same data as the graph above, but even though the information is the same, our eyes see that information differently. When you study this graph, you can follow the line to easily see how the change in rainfall increases and decreases throughout the year.

PICTURE GRAPHS

Here's another handy graph style to use for recording certain kinds of data. This graph shows drawings of the weather. How many totally sunny mornings with no clouds were there in September? How many mornings with rain? It's easy to see the data.

PUTTING DATA TO WORK

1. Use a pen rather than pencil so that original recordings are permanent. Scratch out mistakes with a single line. You may need that information later.

2. Use a bound notebook rather than loose sheets of paper so that no numbers or notes are lost.

3. If you are recording data directly on a computer, be sure to back up the file.

4. Always, _always_ be honest in recording your data, even if the information does not make sense at the time or support your hypothesis. Some of the greatest discoveries were made through accidents or disproven hypotheses.

5. Always put the date at the top of the notebook page where you are recording your data.

WRITE IT DOWN
This young scientist is doing an experiment about air temperature. She has lots of data— both qualitative and quantitative to record.

REVIEW AND DO

REMEMBER THESE CONCEPTS

Observation
"My dog doesn't like his new food. I wonder how it's different?"

Inference
"People are using umbrellas. It must be raining."

Hypothesis
"If I let some of the air out of my soccer ball, then it won't travel as far. "

Experiment
"I am going to try greater amounts of baking soda in my cake recipe to see if the cake rises higher."

Prediction
"I predict that a person can run faster in sneakers than in flip-flops."

Conclusion
"A cleaning solution of vinegar and lemon juice removed stains better than solutions with just one of these ingredients."

REMEMBER THESE MEASUREMENTS

This balance determines the mass of an object by comparing its weight to a known weight.

Length/Distance
- **Millimeters**
- **Centimeters**
- **Meters** • **Kilometers**

Volume
- **Milliliters**
- **Liters**

Mass
- **Grams**
- **Kilograms**

REMEMBER THE DIFFERENCE

Quantitative = Measurements
Qualitative = Other descriptions

REMEMBER THESE GRAPH STYLES

- **Bar Graph**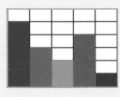
- **Line Graph**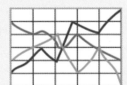
- **Picture Graph**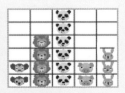

REMEMBER VARIABLES

Independent Variable
Something changed by the experimenter on purpose to see how it affects the outcome.

Dependent Variable
Something that changes in an experiment as a result of the independent variable.

Use pages 10-11 to answer questions 1 and 2.
1. Use your own words to describe each step in the scientific method.
2. Write a definition in your own words for each of the following terms: hypothesis • inference • conclusion

Use pages 12-13 to answer questions 3 and 4.
3. What is the "common language of measurement" used by scientists all over the world? Why do all scientists need to use the same form of measurement?
4. At what Celsius temperature does water boil? Freeze? At what Fahrenheit temperature does water boil? Freeze?

Use pages 14-15 to answer question 5.
5. If Ali added sugar to her experiment, would the sugar be part of the independent variable or dependent variable? Why?

Use pages 16-17 to answer question 6.
6. Explain the difference between quantitative and qualitative data.

THINK LIKE A SCIENTIST

Copy the chart below and sort each observation into the correct category.

Grantsville Elementary School Science Fair

Qualitative Data	Quantitative Data

12 boys, 13 girls • curly hair • 15 fourth graders, 10 fifth graders
brown eyes • wear glasses • 82% belong to the Science Club

DATA DETECTIVE

Create a bar graph showing the data Ali collected during her experiment.
Be sure the graph has a title and labels. Also make sure that the axes are labeled.

Gather the data for the boiling and freezing points of water along with the normal human body temperature in both Fahrenheit and Celsius. Create a chart comparing the two temperature systems.

FORCE, MOTION,

Why does your bike wobble when you start to ride?

How does gravity affect motion?

What is friction?

How do rocket ships take off?

AND ENERGY

CHAPTER 2

LET'S GET PHYSICAL

MAY THE FORCE BE WITH YOU

Physics (*fizz-iks*) is the study of natural phenomena (*fuh-nah-men-uh*). What are phenomena? They are the amazing way nature "works." There is physics involved in the way a pitcher's knuckleball corkscrews toward a batter and the way a car's seatbelt saves lives every day. There is physics at work in a flash of lightning and the buzz of a blender. It is in the design of a sleek race car and the way a rainbow arches across the sky.

A skateboarder's ollie on a half pipe uses physics. So do all the bits and pieces inside your computer. Rockets can soar into space and karate black belts can break bricks and boards with their fists, all thanks to physics—the science that studies energy and the way objects move and react.

AIRBALL!
All sorts of forces are at work on a curveball, from the air hitting the raised stitches, to the circular path of the ball.

BE A PHYSICIST

Physicists (*fizz-uh-sists*) are the scientists who study all the different forces at work in the world. Some physicists work with sound, light, or heat. Others deal with speeding objects and probe the ways things push and pull against one another. Some physicists explore the secrets of vast galaxies on the edges of the known universe. Others work with tiny, mysterious particles that are too small to be seen.

The future of our planet rests in the hands of the next generation of physicists who will have to solve some difficult problems. Will you be one of them?

This physicist works with lasers.

Power and speed are just two of the things physicists study.

There is physics involved in knowing the perfect spot to break a brick.

PROBLEM SOLVING

Physics tries to answer questions about the universe we live in—especially the really hard ones. How do hurricanes form? How are stars born? Is it possible to build a crash-proof car or airplane? Everything we do in our everyday lives involves physics.

KEY WORDS TO KNOW

Force

Any push or pull that causes an object to start, stop, or change speed, direction, or shape.

Energy

The ability to do work.

. . . .

Kinetic Energy

The energy of motion.

. . . .

Potential Energy

Energy that is stored to be used later.

Friction

Resistance to motion created by two objects moving against each other. Friction makes heat.

Speed

How fast and how far an object moves in a certain amount of time. The speed of an object defines the rate of change in its position.

MOTION

From a tiny atom too small to see, to our vast solar system, we live in a world that is constantly in motion. Some things move quickly. Others creep along so slowly you barely know they are moving.

GET A MOVE ON

Have you ever taken a ride on a roller coaster? An amusement park is a great place to learn all about **motion**. As you swoop around, slow down and speed up, or twist to the left or right, you get to experience the science of motion firsthand.

The direction an object is moving and its speed help to describe motion. It is one of the most important parts of physics. Clock hands move in a circular motion. Swings have a back and forth motion. Elevators go up and down.

How fast can something move? What makes something stop moving or change direction? Knowing the answers to these questions can make life safer, easier, and more fun.

START, STOP!

Before you can move, you must have a starting point. The first step in exploring motion is asking yourself exactly where your object is. What is it positioned next to, and what is its relation to its surroundings? You might say, "The pig is next to the barn and the horse is under a tree." Knowing the **location** of an object can be important when doing an experiment.

SPEAK LIKE A SCIENTIST
Motion
A change in the direction, position, or speed of an object.

ON YOUR MARK
When performing an experiment or making a scientific observation, it is important to carefully describe the exact positions and locations of your subjects.

1 2 3 4 5 6 7 8

Speed

The distance an object moves in a certain amount of time. How fast an object is moving.

A stopwatch is used to measure time, which you need to know to find speed.

CHART THE SPEED

What is the best footwear for speedy running? Sami was curious so she conducted an experiment. She had her friend Juan run 100 meters in sneakers. Then she had him run the same distance in flip-flops. Finally, she had him run 100 meters in loafers. She repeated the experiment three times. Here are her results.

The Fastest Footwear

	Trial 1	Trial 2	Trial 3
	16.81 seconds	16.73 seconds	16.86 seconds
	18.41 seconds	17.55 seconds	18.23 seconds
	17.37 seconds	17.23 seconds	17.19 seconds

What footwear was best for running the fastest? Which footwear was the worst? What other variables does she have to consider? What conclusion could Sami make from her experiment?

HOW FAST?

When you think of the word **speed** you probably think of a zooming jet plane or a race car. Scientists use speed data for many purposes. A scientist designing a rocket will need to know how fast the rocket can go and how far it will need to travel in order to design the fuel tanks to power it.

HOW SOON?

When you know the speed of something, you can almost predict the future. You can tell exactly when you will arrive at the movies if you are walking in a straight line at five kilometers an hour. Things get more complicated when objects do not move in a straight line, like a baseball pitcher's curveball, but physicists can figure that out too. A physicist can calculate how long it will take a twisting high diver to reach the water and how much force he will experience as his hands splash in.

There are other things to think about besides speed and motion as we explore the world of physics. What about the diver's mass? And what exactly *is* mass?

How big and how heavy—two important questions to ask as you learn more about motion, force, and energy.

MATTER AND MASS

WHAT DO A HIPPO AND PIZZA HAVE IN COMMON?

They are both made of **matter**. Matter is anything that has mass and takes up space, from the steam pouring out of a hot teapot to a dirty sock, to a brick. Is there anything that is not made of matter? Dreams and emotions—feelings such as happiness, hope, and anger—are a few examples of things that are not made of matter.

THE STATES OF MATTER

Most matter can be sorted into three categories: solids, liquids, and gases. You know that under certain conditions, the state of matter can change. Water can boil and change from a liquid to a gas. It can freeze and change from a liquid to a solid. These changes can cause matter to behave in different ways.

When matter is in a solid state it has a fixed shape that cannot be easily changed. A baseball in your pocket has the exact same amount of matter as that ball hit into left field. Liquids are a little trickier. You can pour a liter of apple juice from a rectangular juice box into a curvy glass and its shape will change a lot, but its matter is the same.

Gases, such as helium and air, are harder to measure. Sometimes you cannot see a gas, but it still has mass. Just blow up a balloon for proof.

Your mass is the same wherever you are—on Earth, on the moon—because the amount of "stuff" you're made of doesn't change, but your weight depends on how much gravity is acting on you. You would weigh much less on the moon than on Earth.

SPEAK LIKE A SCIENTIST

Matter
Anything that has mass and takes up space.

Mass
A measure of how much matter an object has.

WHICH BALL BOWLS BEST?
Size can be misleading. You cannot judge mass by just looking. Even if the beach ball were twice the size of the bowling ball, it would not knock down as many bowling pins because it has less mass.

WHEN MASS MEETS MATTER

Anything that takes up space has **mass**, but the size of something can be very deceiving. Something can take up a lot of space and yet have a small mass, such as a helium-filled parade balloon.

Two objects can be the exact same size, but one can have far more mass. Compare a bowling ball and a beach ball. One is far more densely packed with matter. When it hits something, the object with more mass will have a greater impact. Which ball do you think has more mass?

WHAT ELSE "MATTERS"?

Be it a liquid, solid, or gas—all matter has certain **physical properties** that help describe it. Shape, material, size, and color are some examples of physical properties. Now think about **chemical properties**. Chemical properties describe the way a substance may change or react to form other substances. For example, some metals rust when exposed to air. Paper burns when it meets a lit match.

SOME PROPERTIES OF A CHOCOLATE BAR

Color	Dark brown
Size	15 cm x 7.5 cm x 0.5 cm
Shape	Rectangular
Luster	Slightly shiny
Mass	43 grams
Texture	Smooth
State	Solid. When heated it becomes a thick liquid.

MELTED MATTER
A gooey bar of melted chocolate has the same mass as a solid bar. Which properties describe qualitative data? Quantitative data?

FORCE

Push a grocery cart. Pull a wagon. Stop a car. Turn left or right. What makes the world move?

SPEAK LIKE A SCIENTIST

Force

Any push or pull that causes an object to change speed, direction, or shape.

MAY THE FORCE BE WITH YOU

Imagine trying to push an elephant. You would not be able to get it to budge. You are small and light compared to the elephant, which is big and very heavy. Now imagine this: You are trying to kick a soccer ball. You are heavy compared to the light ball. If you kick it, it will move easily. **Force** is the word we use to describe a push or pull that makes an object move, stop moving, speed up, or change direction. Physicists discovered several "laws" about motion. These **laws of motion** also involve force and speed.

BIG OBJECT, SMALL FORCE
Moving a heavy elephant will take a lot more force than this small boy can exert.

The more massive an object, the harder it is to force it to move.

To put it simply: An enormous elephant will not be moved by a fourth grader even if the student pushes with all of his or her strength.

The greater the force, the greater the change in motion will be.

To put it simply: If an enormous elephant pushes a fourth grader, that student is going to go flying!

FORCE-FULL

Think of all the different forces you face each day. You will have to use force every time you open or close a door. You might have to walk against the force of a strong wind. You used force to pull your backpack off the floor and onto your shoulders. The force of your foot pushing against the pavement sends your scooter or skateboard speeding down the street. Force is at work in many ways.

Keep a "Forces Journal" for one hour. Record every time you use a force and every time a force is used against you. Push away from the dinner table, pull open a drawer, get nudged by your pet—write it all down.

HANDS-ON SCIENCE

TESTING THE LAWS OF FORCE AND MOTION

1. Set up three empty milk cartons. Take a piece of notebook paper and wad it into a ball. Roll the paper at the milk cartons. What happened? Now repeat the experiment with a baseball or other heavier ball. What happened this time? Explain why.

2. Grab a beach ball, blow it up, and go outside. Make sure you are in an open space. Flick the ball with your finger and measure how far it traveled. Now swat it with an open hand and measure the distance it moves. What happened? Which law of motion did you demonstrate?

3. Do you have a pair of roller skates? A skateboard? Put on your helmet, then grab a ball. Stand on your skateboard or strap on your skates and then throw the ball as hard as you can. What happens? Which of the three laws of motion did you demonstrate?

OPPOSITES

There is another law of motion that involves force. The next time you go ice-skating or rollerblading with a friend, face each other and push your palms against your friend's palms, as hard as you can. What happens? Even though you are pushing *toward* each other, you will move away from your friend.

> **For every action, there is an equal and opposite reaction.**

This law of motion is what propels rockets into outer space. Hot gases are pushed out from the bottom of the rocket, which makes the rocket thrust upward. The force of all the gases pushing downward from the rocket is the exact opposite of the force with which the rocket moves skyward.

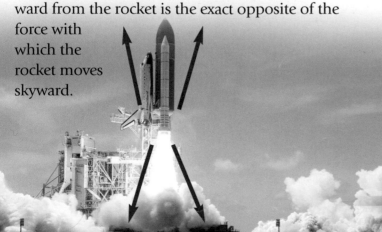

SCIENCE IN EVERYDAY LIFE

When a person slams on the brakes while driving, the car slows down and stops. But <u>*you*</u> *do not have brakes. If you were not wearing a seatbelt you would continue to move. The seatbelt works as a strong force to stop you from going through the windshield.*

GRAVITY

Without it, dogs would fly, trees would uproot, and the whole world would be topsy-turvy.

IN A WORLD WITHOUT GRAVITY...
Things would be floating all over the place. It would be almost impossible to control your movements.

A POWERFUL PULL

Gravity is one of the most important forces in the universe. It keeps our planet revolving around the sun instead of hurtling off into the dark, bleak edges of outer space. It is what keeps us from floating into the clouds. It is why, when you knock a book off your desk, it falls *down* instead of *up*.

Gravity is a pulling force that exists across the deepest reaches of space. Gravity is always at work. Here on Earth it is constantly pulling objects downward toward the core of our planet. Gravity is the reason why you will weigh a certain amount when you step on a bathroom scale. Gravity is pulling your **mass** down onto that scale.

Objects with a very large mass have a greater pull than objects with small masses. Our sun has a huge mass—much greater than the Earth's. Gravity is what keeps the Earth and the other planets in their orbits around the sun.

SPEAK LIKE A SCIENTIST
Gravity
A pulling force between objects. The more massive the object, the stronger the pull.

If the sun has so much gravity, why aren't we pulled off of the surface of the Earth and sucked towards the sun? The strength of the gravitational force that you feel also depends on the distance between objects. You are MUCH closer to the Earth than you are to the sun, so Earth's gravity keeps your feet firmly on the ground.

WEIGHTLESS!

There is gravity everywhere in the universe. Consider our moon. The Earth's gravity keeps the moon from flying away. So why do astronauts on the moon feel almost weightless? A 70 kg astronaut still has the exact same mass (or "stuff" inside him) on the moon, but he can jump higher and feels much lighter. Why? His *weight* has changed. Remember, weight and mass are different. Mass is the amount of matter in you. Weight is the force of gravity pulling on your mass. The moon has less mass than the Earth and, therefore, has less gravity, so there is not as much force pulling a person down toward the surface of the moon. Astronauts feel lighter. In space, far away from any big planets, they would feel "weightless"!

> *One important law of motion states:*
> **Unless acted on by a force,**
> **objects in motion tend to stay in motion**
> **and objects at rest stay at rest.**

These heavy weights have a lot of mass. Putting them in motion takes a lot of effort.

BARELY MOVING

Scientists use the word **inertia** to describe how easy it is to keep matter moving once it is in motion. They use the same word to describe how hard it is to get an object to move if it is "at rest" or not moving. Massive things, like enormous tree trunks and heavy boulders, have greater inertia than pebbles or raisins. Something with a lot of inertia is very hard to start or stop moving. Think of playing with a toy wagon. When it is empty, it's easy to pull down the road. When two friends jump in the wagon, you must flex your muscles and add much more force to get that wagon going!

THE LAW OF INERTIA IN ACTION

Have you ever noticed that when you first begin pedaling your bike it is very wobbly, but as you gain speed it becomes more stable? Every time you ride your bike you are demonstrating an important law of motion. Your bike was at rest when you got on it. It will stay that way without an input of force. As you start pedaling you are working to overcome inertia. That is why you wobble.

Now imagine you are riding your bike at a speed of 14 km per hour. You and your bike are in motion—that is until you hit a large log in the road. Your bike has been acted upon by a force. Your bike will stop suddenly and you may end up, face down, on the pavement. Because you stayed in motion, you have had a painful experience with the law of inertia.

FRICTION

What happens when two objects rub against each other? Things get hot!

RUB-A-DUB-DUB

Have you ever come inside on a cold day and rubbed your hands together to warm them up? The warmth you felt came from **friction** (_frick-shun_)—a force you make use of every time you walk down the street.

SKIP THE SLIP

When two objects rub against each other there is always resistance. The resistance to motion causes an effect. It makes heat. That's friction!

What would life be like without friction? Imagine walking on a sheet of slippery ice. You would be sliding every which way. Roads and sidewalks have more friction than an ice rink. Friction helps keep cars securely on the road instead of skidding all over the place.

BUMPY!

How does friction work? Even things that look smooth, such as a tabletop and a cup bottom, have microscopic lumps and bumps. As any two surfaces move against each other, all the little lumps collide. This slows the motion of the objects. At the same time, it also creates heat from all the rubbing. Things like sneaker bottoms and car tires have lots of extra bumps to provide more friction for a better grip.

THREE EXAMPLES OF FRICTION

• The soles of your shoes create friction with the floor. Friction wears away at your shoe bottoms.

• Pencil erasers work by creating friction. Friction removes the pencil marks.

• Blisters occur when too-tight shoes create friction with the skin on your heels or toes.

CAN YOU FEEL THE FRICTION?

Some materials create greater friction than others. Try these experiments with friction.

1. Take a smooth rubber ball and a tennis ball and try spinning each one in a bowl of water. Which spins the most times? Which spins the fastest? Why do you think this happened?

2. You will need three identical 8" square foil brownie pans.

- Fill one with 2.5 cm of water and put it in the freezer overnight.
- Lay a sheet of sandpaper or a carpet scrap on the bottom of the second pan.
- Place a smooth piece of aluminum foil on the bottom of the third.
- Push a small shirt button across the surfaces of each. Which had the least friction? Which had the most? What other surfaces do you think would have a lot of friction?

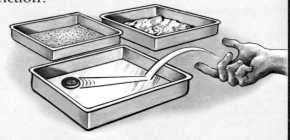

Olympic swimmers often wear special swimsuits that reduce the friction between cloth and the water to help them swim faster.

FIGHTING FRICTION

Sometimes friction can create problems. Car engines have several metal parts that rub against one another. One of the reasons we have to add oil to car engines is to help protect against the damage that all that rubbing would create. Oil fills in the spaces between the lumps and bumps to provide a smoother surface so the friction is reduced. Can you think of any other surfaces that rub together? Where might friction be a problem?

LINK TO THE PAST

One of humankind's great triumphs was the discovery of friction and how to use it to make fires. But starting a fire is not easy, so the American Indians depended on a simple fire starter—a wooden tool with two parts: a flat board with small holes carved in it and a stick.

Twirling the stick quickly by holding it between your palms and rubbing your hands together allows friction to build up. Heat is created and makes sparks. If you add some dried grass or flakes of bark, which can easily catch fire, it won't be long before you are roasting a turkey leg on a spit.

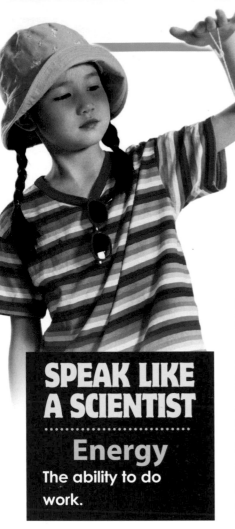

TWO KINDS OF ENERGY

Have ever played with a yo-yo or kicked a soccer ball? If you have, you have done "work." Your work has transferred energy to an object and made it move.

Energy helps airplanes fly and bakes gooey cookies. But even a rock sitting on a hillside is full of energy. That's because there are two kinds of energy.

All moving objects have **kinetic** *(kin-eh-tick)* **energy**. Objects in motion—a stone rolling down a hillside, a roaring campfire, a soccer ball flying toward the goal—are releasing all that kinetic energy. Another kind of energy is called **potential** *(poe-ten-shul)* **energy**. Potential energy is energy that is stored, just waiting to be used, like a rock atop a hillside, waiting to slide down. Imagine the moment when a roller coaster car reaches the tip-top of an incline just before it starts down. It is filled with potential energy that will be released and turned into kinetic energy as it hurtles down the track.

SPEAK LIKE A SCIENTIST

Energy
The ability to do work.

POTENTIAL ENERGY

Here are some examples:

• A rubber band that has been stretched as far as it can go.

• A bow that has been pulled back with an arrow resting on it, ready to release.

• The electrical energy stored in the batteries in a remote control that is not being used.

• A roller coaster car that is at the top of the highest peak seconds before it starts to drop.

KINETIC ENERGY

Here are some examples:

• A rubber band that has been released and is now shooting across the room.

• An arrow that has just been shot and is zooming toward its target.

• A battery-operated television remote control being used to change stations.

• A roller coaster car as it speeds downward along the track.

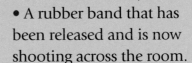

Dry firewood is full of potential energy. When lit it releases kinetic energy in the form of heat and light.

WORKING TOGETHER

Where does kinetic energy come from? For snowboarders, the potential energy that they have at the top of a snowy hill turns into kinetic energy as they race to the bottom. Energy is actually changing from one type to another all the time. Heat, light, motion, and sound are all examples of energy. The water in a lake at the top of a dam has a lot of potential energy. When the water is allowed to move over the dam, its potential energy turns into kinetic energy. This energy can even be used to generate electricity! Can you think of any other examples of energy changing?

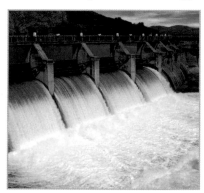

HANDS-ON SCIENCE

HOT RUBBER

Rubber bands are a great way to experiment with potential and kinetic energy.

1. Hold a rubber band against your cheek. Does it feel warm? Cool? Now stretch and release the rubber band ten times. Hold it against your cheek again. How did it feel? Why did it feel warmer? Where did the warmth come from?

2. Gather a dozen rubber bands. Be sure they are different in length and width. Now clear an area and start shooting them in the same direction, making sure that no one or thing is in the way. Which traveled the farthest? Which had the most potential energy stored within it?

3. Grab a lunch bag with a handle. Now snip a rubber band so it looks like an elastic string. Tie one end to the handle of the bag. On an uncarpeted floor, gently start moving the bag towards you by pulling on the rubber band. What happened? Did the rubber band have to stretch more at first to get the bag to move? What happened once the bag was moving?

Slingshots use the release of potential energy to propel an object across a distance.

REVIEW AND DO

MOTION
describes an object's path, direction, and speed.

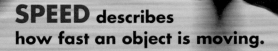

SPEED describes how fast an object is moving.

FORCE is any push or pull that causes an object to move, stop, or change direction or shape.

FRICTION
is the resistance to motion that occurs when two objects move against each other.

ENERGY CAN EXIST IN TWO STATES

KINETIC: energy being released.

POTENTIAL: energy being stored.

Use pages 24-25 to answer questions 1 and 2.

1. Look at the picture of the runners at the bottom of page 24. In complete sentences, describe the runner in lane one's location in relation to track markings, other runners, and any geographic feature.

2. What is speed? What scientific tool can you use to gather data to help calculate speed?

Use pages 26-27 to answer question 3.

3. What is the difference between matter and mass?

Use pages 28-29 to answer questions 4 and 5.

4. Any push or pull that causes an object to move, stop, or change speed and direction is called _____.

5. Will a kindergarten student kicking a soccer ball or a teacher kicking a soccer ball create the greater change in the motion of the soccer ball? Why? Which law of motion does this show?

Use pages 32-33 to answer question 6.

6. Explain why the author chose to use a picture of a match and matchbox to illustrate friction.

Use pages 34-35 to complete question 7.

7. Copy and complete the graphic organizer below by defining each term.

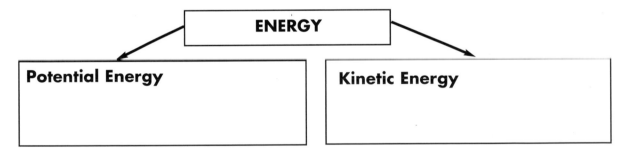

THINK LIKE A SCIENTIST

Design an experiment to test one of the laws of motion.

DATA DETECTIVE

Jody tested how far a toy car would travel on different surfaces when flicked with a finger. On what surface did the car travel the farthest? The least far? What can you infer about the friction of each surface?

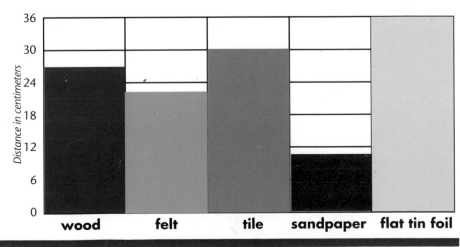

Surface Types

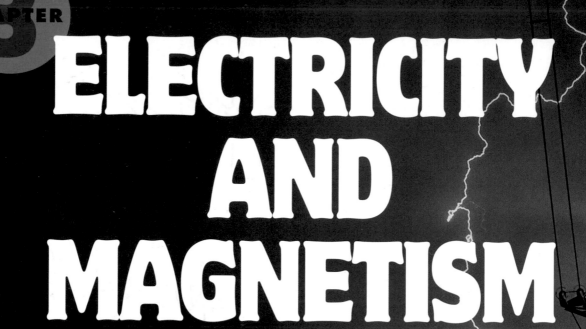

CHAPTER 3

ELECTRICITY AND MAGNETISM

Why do we get shocked?

What is lightning?

How is electricity made?

How can magnets create electricity?

POWERING UP

Imagine life without electric lights, television, or computers. No toasters, microwaves, or video games. We depend on electricity for so many things! But what exactly *is* electricity?

LET THERE BE LIGHT

Kinetic and potential energy are two kinds of energy, but there is another way we use the word "energy." If we can somehow capture energy, we can use it as a power source. **Electricity** *(ee-lek-tri-sit-ee)* is a perfect example.

A world without electricity would be a much duller, dimmer place. Fortunately some hard-working scientists had some very "bright" ideas. They knew there were forces of energy at work in the world. All they had to do was figure out how to put them to work.

300 YEARS OF PROGRESS

For thousands of years, candlelight and oil lamps were how people lit their homes, but in the 1700s all that began to change as several scientists began experimenting with electricity. They learned how to make batteries. They then combined electricity with magnets, which led to a wonderful new invention—the electric motor.

By 1809 the very first lightbulb lit up a room for a few brief, bright minutes before sizzling off. It would be 70 more years before a longer-lasting lightbulb would be invented and scientists learned how to provide a safe, steady supply of electricity into people's homes. Let's flick a switch and learn more about all things electric!

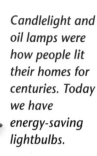

Candlelight and oil lamps were how people lit their homes for centuries. Today we have energy-saving lightbulbs.

BE AN ELECTRICAL ENGINEER

* * * * * * * * * * * * *

The scientists who work with circuits, electrical current, and electromagnets create all sorts of awesome things such as smartphones, robots, computers, and video game players. Electrical engineers like to say, "If I can dream it, I can make it."

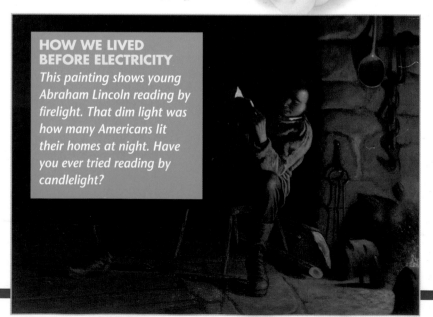

HOW WE LIVED BEFORE ELECTRICITY
This painting shows young Abraham Lincoln reading by firelight. That dim light was how many Americans lit their homes at night. Have you ever tried reading by candlelight?

KEY WORDS FOR ELECTRICITY

Electricity

A form of energy made by electrons.
There are two kinds of electrical energy.

Current Electricity

The flow of free electrons along a
pathway such as a wire.

*Sparks travel
between two wires.*

Static Electricity

Electrons that do not flow, but build
up on a material.

BAD HAIR DAY
*This girl has touched
a Vandergraff
generator—a
machine that stores
static electricity.*

Circuit

The pathway
on which
current
travels.

*A simple
circuit*

Insulators

*Rubber
coating*

Materials that do not allow
electricity to flow.

Conductors

Materials that allow electrical
currents to pass more easily.

*Copper
wire*

...AND MAGNETISM

Magnetism
(*mag-nuh-tiz-um*)

A force that
can attract or
repel certain
substances.

Electromagnet
(*ee-lek-trow-mag-net*)

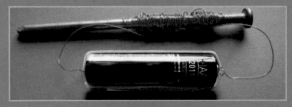

A magnet created by the flow of
electric current.

41

ELECTRONS AT WORK

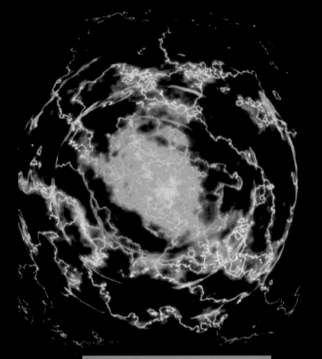

We use electrical energy to power machines and to heat and light our homes. But what is it? Where does it come from?

To understand electricity we have to go deep into the unseen world—a world where only powerful microscopes can see things.

Imagine a small speck of gold. Now imagine breaking it into smaller and smaller pieces. Keep making it smaller until you need a very powerful microscope to see the bits. At a certain point, you will reach the gold's **atoms**.

An atom is a tiny bit of matter. Remember—matter is anything that has mass and takes up space. Many things in the universe are made from different combinations of matter, but certain things, such as gold, silver, and iron, are not made of combinations. They are simply one thing.

ELECTRONS AT WORK
This image shows the movement of a cloud of electrons around a helium nucleus. The colors show the action of helium's four electrons.

THE ELECTRIC MR. EDISON

It is hard to believe that one of the greatest geniuses of all time was kicked out of school because his teachers thought he was "addled" —not very smart! Taught at home by his mother, Thomas Edison (1847–1931) spent a lot of time reading and tinkering and eventually made many contributions to the harnessing of electricity—putting all those tiny sparks to use. Edison, who was almost deaf, began doing lots of experiments with sound. He eventually invented the first phonograph—a machine that plays recorded music. But we remember him for one particularly "bright" invention that changed our lives: a better lightbulb.

Edison did not invent the lightbulb, but in 1879, after testing 3,000 different materials, he invented a lightbulb that would burn for a very long time—not just a few minutes like previous ones. More importantly, because lightbulbs need electricity, in 1882 Edison developed the world's first power station, which supplied users with a steady, safe source of electricity. What good is the lightbulb if there is no electricity to turn it on?

Over the next 50 years, Edison's workshop in Menlo Park, New Jersey, became the birthplace of almost two thousand life-changing inventions, from motion pictures to better batteries. The "Wizard of Menlo Park" got his 1,093rd, and last, patent (patents are a way to protect a unique invention) at age 83. His legacy? He left the world a much brighter place!

INSIDE AN ATOM

There are gold atoms and silver atoms, hydrogen atoms and copper atoms, but all atoms have one thing in common. They are made of three parts—**protons** (<u>pro</u>-tonz), **neutrons** (<u>new</u>-tronz), and **electrons** (ee-<u>lek</u>-tronz). What makes them different is the number of protons and electrons each type of atom has.

The center of the atom is called the **nucleus** (<u>new</u>-klee-us). The nucleus is a bit like our sun, sitting in the middle of our solar system. A nucleus is made of a bundle of protons and neutrons. Now imagine clumps of clouds surrounding the nucleus. These are the electrons. Electrons—and the way they behave—are an important part of **electricity**.

ELECTRONS AND ELECTRICITY

Each part of the atom has a different electrical charge. Protons have a positive charge (**+**). Electrons have a negative charge (**-**). Neutrons have no charge. The protons and neutrons hug each other, but the electrons zip around and around. Sometimes electrons even escape from their cloud and travel to another atom.

ELECTRONS ON THE MOVE

Have you ever snapped two magnets together? Do you remember how it felt as they were pulled toward one another? Negatively charged electrons do the same thing when they are around a positive charge like a proton. To understand electricity, you need to know that electrons in one area are attracted to protons in another area. They need a pathway to travel along from their negative areas to the positive area. We call that path a **circuit** (<u>sir</u>-kit).

Electricity flows by the motion of electrons in a circuit. When there is a good path, there is a constant flow of negatively charged electrons and an electric current occurs.

Electricity is the name we use to describe nature's big and little sparks, as well as our most widely used energy source. Read on to learn how we put it to use in our everyday lives.

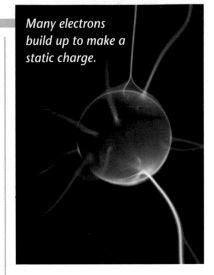

Many electrons build up to make a static charge.

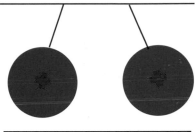

These protons push away from each other. They both have a positive charge.

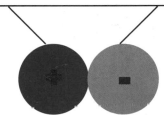

The negative charge of the electron wants to snap together with the positive charge of the proton because they are different charges.

In some materials, particularly metals, the electrons farthest from the nucleus can move freely from one atom to another. Electricity is the flow of these free electrons along a pathway such as a wire.

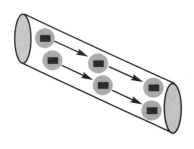

STATIC ELECTRICITY

There is electricity all around us. Sometimes it is annoying, other times it is dangerous. For centuries, the big question was "How can it be made useful?"

I AM SHOCKED!

Have you ever found a sock stuck to your shirt after emptying the clothes dryer? What makes sparks fly when you walk across a carpet and then touch a metal doorknob? Why does pulling off a wool or fleece cap on a cold, dry day make your hair stand straight up? These all happen because of **static** (*sta-tick*) **electricity**. Static electricity happens when electrons do not flow, and build up on a material.

A HAIR-RAISING EXPERIENCE

Let's take a closer look at those standing-up hairs. In the winter, removing your wool hat rubs it against your hair. Electrons move from your hair to the hat. This also happens when you rub a balloon on your head. Now your hairs have an imbalance of positive and negative charges. The hairs are now *very* positive.

Since materials with the same charge repel (push away from) each other, the hairs on your body try to get as far from each other as possible. The farthest they can get is by standing up and pushing away from all the other strands. Talk about a bad hair day!

Why do we notice static electricity more during the winter? During the summer, the air is more humid. The water in the air helps electrons leap off you more quickly, so you can't build up much of a charge. In the winter, the air is so dry that electrons can really build up. Touch a doorknob and they all leap off at once. ZAP!

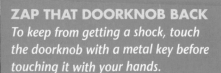

ZAP THAT DOORKNOB BACK
To keep from getting a shock, touch the doorknob with a metal key before touching it with your hands.

44

THE ON-OFF SWITCH

Static electricity cannot power up a TV set or make a steady light source. That is because the electrons are not flowing. They are just sitting there. Electrons must flow for an appliance to work. That's called a **current**. The electricity that flows from the power station through your home's electrical outlets and into your appliances is current electricity. When most people say "electricity" they are thinking of current electricity—the flow of electrons along a path.

PUTTING STATIC TO WORK

Getting an electric shock is pretty annoying, but static can be very useful. Have you ever made a Xerox or similar kind of photocopy? Those machines use static electricity to do their work. Some copy machines electrically charge the ink so that it will stick to the paper. Other copiers leave an electrical charge on the rollers that deliver the ink.

Many automobile makers use the power of static electricity in their spray painting machines. These help direct the paint to the target without waste, leading to a better paint job.

REALLY BIG STATIC

On steamy, stormy, summer nights you will sometimes see a hot bolt of white light streak through the sky. That bolt is **lightning**—the release, or discharge, of a large amount of static electricity into the atmosphere. These powerful bolts can reach temperatures of more than 20,000 degrees Celsius and are sometimes over 160 kilometers in length. On average, over 20 million lightning flashes strike the U.S. every year.

A huge fork of lightning can be hotter than the surface of the sun.

FRANKLIN'S FIND

Franklin probably never flew a kite with a key attached in a storm and neither should you!

Did Benjamin Franklin (1706–1790) really run outside and fly a kite with a metal key dangling from it in the middle of a lightning storm? Probably not, but this amazing man of science—one of the greatest thinkers ever—made a big contribution to the understanding of electricity by proving that lightning is an electrical current that exists in nature.

Franklin went on to invent all sorts of awesome devices to protect us from lightning. He devised the lightning rod—a tall metal pole that attracts lightning and keeps it from striking people and homes, where it could start fires. He also invented lightning bells, which could sense the presence of electricity in the air and ring out a warning.

He remained fascinated by all things electric throughout his long, amazing life and was one of the world's greatest scientists.

INSULATORS

How do electrons move? How can we use electricity and not get constant painful shocks?

Have you ever noticed that your toaster cord is wrapped in a layer of rubber or plastic? That wrapping allows you to touch the cord without getting shocked by current electricity.

Plastic, rubber, wood, and glass are all examples of good **insulators**. These materials block the flow of electrons. Electrons cannot easily move through them. Often you will see wires made from metals such as copper wrapped in a layer of rubber or plastic. This insulation keeps the electrons from escaping. A **resistor**—such as a wire inside a lightbulb— slows the flow of electrons down, allowing only some to pass.

CONDUCTORS

How can we get electricity to our cell phone and other electrical devices?

Some materials allow electricity to easily travel across them. They are like superhighways for electrons to speed through. These are called **conductors**. Metals such as steel, copper, iron, gold, and silver are all great conductors.

Travel down most roads and you will see long lengths of wire stretching for miles. These long wires carry electricity from the places where it is generated to our homes, schools, and workplaces. The wires keep America's electric supply flowing.

Thin conducting strands of copper wire are twisted together, and then wrapped in an insulating layer of rubber.

SPEAK LIKE A SCIENTIST

Insulator
(*in*-suh-*lay*-tur)

Any material that reduces or prevents the flow of electricity, heat, cold, or sound.

Conductor
(cun-*duck*-tur)

Any material that allows the flow of electricity, heat, cold, or sound.

Circuit
(*sir*-kut)

A device that provides a pathway for the flow of electrons, allowing for the movement of electricity.

CIRCUITS

A circuit delivers electricity from a power source to a lightbulb, buzzer, or motor.

Flashlights, blenders, fans, and doorbells all have something in common. They are examples of things that are powered by simple **circuits**. Some circuits use electricity from power stations. Others use it from batteries, which are sometimes called **dry cells**.

A dry cell battery is a container full of chemicals that react with one another to become a source of electrons.

Every dry cell has a positive and negative end. When you link the two ends with a wire, electrons are able to flow in a circuit.

The inside of a dry cell

PICTURE THIS...

Every day, delivery vans pick up packages at a warehouse and deliver them along a set route to their destinations. If the roads are blocked, the vans cannot make their delivery.

Electric circuits are a lot like those delivery vans. They pick up electrons and take them along a "roadway" of wire to the place where they deliver energy. An on-off switch is a lot like a roadblock that stops traffic. After the vans have made their delivery, another imaginary truck will arrive bringing more electrons to repeat the process.

ROAD CLOSED

A CIRCLE OF LIGHT

A circuit is the link between a power supply, such as a battery, and the item waiting to be powered—things such as lightbulbs, buzzers, or motors. In order for a circuit to work, the wires that form the circuit have to go in a full loop from the power source to the lightbulb and back to the power source. If there is any break in the circuit, electricity will not continue to flow.

Switches allow you to open or close a circuit. When the switch is set to the ON position, the circuit is complete. A switch to the OFF position breaks the circuit. Just like a washed away bridge or a big roadblock, the "load," in this case electricity, cannot get delivered.

EVERY DAY IN MANY WAYS

Think about all the items with on-off switches you use in a day. Keep track of how many times in one 24-hour period you turn something on and off. How many things with an on-off switch run on batteries? How many of those need to be plugged in to be recharged?

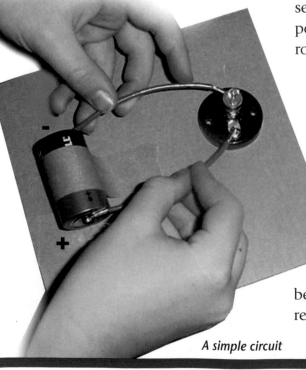
A simple circuit

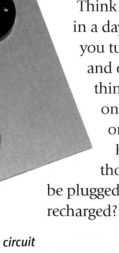

Our modern world depends on electricity for thousands of things.

BUILDING CIRCUITS

Lighting a single lightbulb is a simple task. Lighting an entire classroom calls for a different solution.

Many years ago, holiday lights were very difficult to use. Just one bad bulb in the string of light meant none of the lights worked. It all had to do with the type of circuit. There are three basic kinds of circuits.

Think back to the description of the "delivery van" delivering "packages." The electricity is stored in a "warehouse"—a dry cell or a power station. The delivery van carries the electricity along a "roadway," which is the wire system. If you have two delivery vans, you can deliver more packages, right? If you have two roadways to travel along, you don't have to worry about any "traffic jams." The three types of circuits shown here use different combinations of a roadway, a delivery system, and the number of drop-off points to deliver electricity to a device.

A KEY FOR DRAWING CIRCUITS

Looks like this — *Draw it like this*

Bulb

Dry cell

Switch

1. SIMPLE CIRCUIT

A simple circuit has one power source, one lightbulb, and one switch. A switch makes a simple circuit much easier to use. Without a switch you would have to keep disconnecting a wire to turn it off.

OPEN CIRCUIT

CLOSED CIRCUIT

2. SERIES CIRCUITS

The series circuit (below) has two or more bulbs being powered. One switch turns on both lights.

You might find this type of circuit (batteries lined up) used in a flashlight.

These bulbs have to share the power, therefore they do not glow as brightly as a circuit with one bulb.

If one bulb breaks, then the circuit is broken, and neither bulb will light.

This kind of series circuit has two or more power sources for one bulb.

This bulb will glow more brightly than a circuit with one battery, but it will shine for the same length of time.

You might find this type of circuit used in a string of old-fashioned Christmas lights.

3. PARALLEL (SIDE-BY-SIDE) CIRCUITS

This kind of parallel circuit has two separate paths bringing electricity to the bulbs.

If one bulb breaks, the other one will still light up because it has its own path for electrons to flow.

This kind of parallel circuit has the dry cells side by side. This will power a device for twice as long as a simple circuit.

This bulb will stay lit twice as long and will shine just as brightly as the simple circuit.

You might find this type of circuit used to light your home. One switch and one power source control several lights.

You might find this type of circuit (batteries side by side) in a wireless mouse or a TV remote.

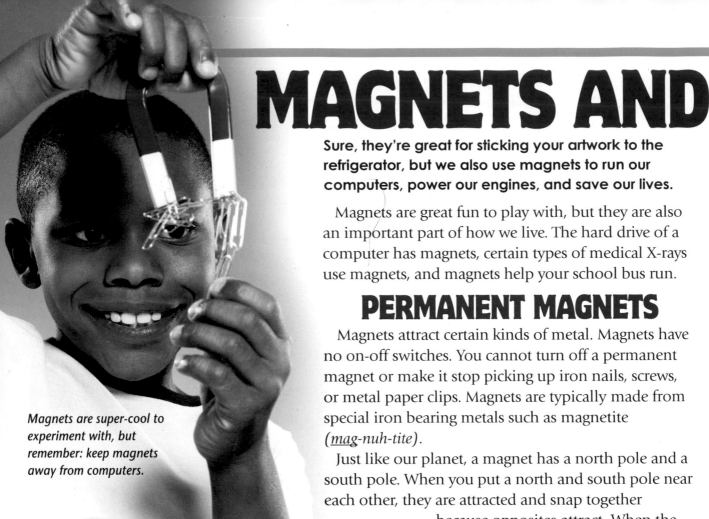

MAGNETS AND

Sure, they're great for sticking your artwork to the refrigerator, but we also use magnets to run our computers, power our engines, and save our lives.

Magnets are great fun to play with, but they are also an important part of how we live. The hard drive of a computer has magnets, certain types of medical X-rays use magnets, and magnets help your school bus run.

PERMANENT MAGNETS

Magnets attract certain kinds of metal. Magnets have no on-off switches. You cannot turn off a permanent magnet or make it stop picking up iron nails, screws, or metal paper clips. Magnets are typically made from special iron bearing metals such as magnetite (_mag-nuh-tite_).

Just like our planet, a magnet has a north pole and a south pole. When you put a north and south pole near each other, they are attracted and snap together because opposites attract. When the poles match (north-north or south-south) they repel each other and push apart. No matter how hard you try to force them together they will not attract.

Magnets are super-cool to experiment with, but remember: keep magnets away from computers.

LINK TO THE PAST

In a part of ancient Greece called Magnesia, people knew that a particular kind of rock attracted bits of iron. The special rock became known as magnetite. This is where we get the words magnet and magnetism.

The ancient Chinese also had deposits of this amazing stone, and they also put it to work. They discovered that if you took a splinter of magnetite and put it on something that could spin, it would always end up pointing north— information that would be useful when they traveled. They had invented the first compass.

These magnets are pushing away from each other because the same poles are facing each other.

European explorers put the compass to good use as they began to sail the Earth's seas.

A Chinese compass. Think about ways this invention would have helped the Chinese as they built their great empire thousands of years ago.

MAGNETISM

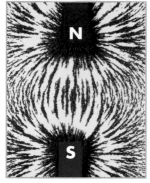

These magnets have the north and south poles facing each other. The magnets attract.

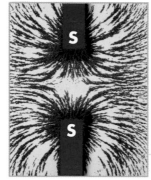

These magnets have both south poles facing each other. The magnets repel.

A SWIRL OF POWER
When you drop metal bits around a bar magnet, you can clearly see an arched pattern that forms. Can you follow the magnetic field of this magnet?

UNSEEN FORCES

Magnetism is an invisible force but there is a way to see its effects. If you scatter small iron shavings along a magnet, an interesting pattern appears. **Lines of force** extend from the poles of a magnet in an arched pattern. These lines show the area that a magnet's force reaches—the **magnetic field**. What causes it? The magnet is reaching out to other magnets or magnetic materials that might be in the area.

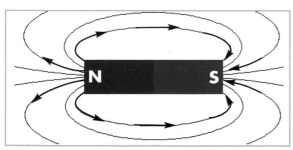

Here's how to draw a magnetic field. The arcs flow from north to south.

MAGNETIC MEDICINE
MRIs use magnetic fields to create images of the inside of the human body. A doctor can see how badly and where this ankle was broken.

PUTTING MAGNETS TO WORK

Magnets are used for a lot more than just toys. There are magnets in many of the appliances in your home, from your actual refrigerator (not just the plastic pizza magnets stuck to the door), to your blender, to the family car. A computer uses magnets to record data on the hard drive. Loudspeakers and headphones use magnets. Doctors depend on MRIs (*magnetic resonance imaging*) to see deep inside the human body, and trash recyclers use magnets to help them sort valuable scrap metal from other garbage.

Electricity and magnets are closely linked. In fact, anything that has an electric motor depends on magnets to make it run. Find out how on the next page.

ELECTROMAGNETISM

Magnets are great, but a magnet that can be controlled is even better!

OFF-AND-ON MAGNETS

About 200 years ago, a very smart scientist discovered that when you pass an electric current through a coil of wire, that wire becomes magnetic. We call this kind of magnet an **electromagnet**. This is a kind of magnetism that can be controlled. It can be turned on and off, and made more powerful or weaker. The discovery of this amazing new invention changed life all across the world.

SPEAK LIKE A SCIENTIST

Electromagnet

(ee-lek-tro-mag-nit)

A magnet made by wrapping wire around an iron core. When current flows through the wire the iron becomes a magnet.

MAKE YOUR OWN MAGNET
All it takes is these items.

MAKE AN ELECTRO-MAGNET

HANDS-ON SCIENCE

No need to go digging for magnetite. You can make and test a magnet with these five things. You will need:

1 iron nail about 6" long
3 meters (10 feet) of 22-gauge coated copper wire (insulated)
1 rubber band
1 dry cell—size AA, C, or D
15 metal paper clips

• Stretch out the copper wire and fold it in half to make two strands. Take the iron nail and begin to neatly wrap the copper wire around it 10 times—5 wraps of each strand—starting at the midpoint, leaving the extra wire at each end.

• Use a rubber band to secure each end of the wire to the + and - ends of a dry cell.
• When the wire ends are attached, try to pick up some metal paper clips. What happens?

• Now try wrapping the copper wire 20 times more before hooking up your battery. Did it pick up more paper clips?
• Try wrapping the copper wire 30 times more before hooking up your battery. Now what happened?
• What conclusions can you draw from wrapping more wire?

FROM ELECTROMAGNETS TO ELECTRICITY

Moving magnetic fields do something amazing. They push electrons. Metals such as copper have electrons that are very "jumpy" and can easily be pushed around by moving magnets. The flow of all those electrons creates electricity. But now what?

By using moving magnets and copper wire together, you can generate a steady stream of electricity. You just learned that when you run electricity through a coil of wire that is wrapped around an iron core, it creates an electromagnet. What if you put that electromagnet on an axle so that it could spin, and then put everything inside a tube with magnets stuck all around it? By adding a few other parts, you can put this to work by creating a very simple motor.

Your electromagnet will push against the magnetic fields of the magnets on the tube and start to move. A few extra parts are needed to keep it spinning in the same direction. You might attach a wheel or some fan blades to the axle, and they will spin too. Electrical energy will be converted into mechanical energy. That's how most of the electrical appliances in your house work. When you turn off the power, the electromagnet is no longer magnetic, and the coil stops spinning. Your appliance is now "off."

Electric motors use something called an armature. Can you see all the wire coiled inside this one? If the field of the electromagnet flips at the exact right moment, the armature (which powers a motor) will spin freely.

JUNKYARD WORKER
Huge electromagnets are great for finding valuable scrap metal that can be recycled.

THE FANTASTIC MR. FARADAY

Without Michael Faraday (1791–1867), Thomas Edison might never have created so many great inventions! This English scientist made one of the most important discoveries in the field of electricity.

Faraday was one of the first people to figure out that a magnetic field could produce a steady stream of electricity. Faraday used that knowledge to invent the first electric generator—a machine that creates usable electricity—and with it, the electric motor.

Most of Faraday's experiments ended in failure, but this humble scientist always said he learned as much from failure as from success. That is wonderful advice for every scientist to remember, straight from the "father of electronics."

PUTTING ELECTRICAL ENERGY TO WORK

How do you take electrical energy and turn it into heat, light, or mechanical energy?

Flick on a light switch in your house and a lamp will light up. But where does that electricity come from? How do we capture all those wandering electrons and make them run our toasters?

A VISIT TO A POWER PLANT

Have you ever heard a whistling tea kettle? As the water boils, it makes steam. Powerful clouds of steam have the ability to move things. Much of our electric supply gets it start with boiling water in power plants all over the country.

Most power plants in the United States burn fuels such as coal, gas, or oil to heat water, which creates steam. These powerful clouds of steam push special machines called turbines which spin magnets to help create electricity.

The Clover Power Station in Halifax County, Virginia, uses coal to generate electricity.

FROM STEAM TO POWER

1. In a coal plant, hot coals heat giant pots of water.

2. The steam from the boiling water spins a turbine. A turbine is a motor driven by water, steam, or wind to create electrical energy.

3. The turbine powers a generator—a device that spins a magnet near a coil of wire to create a steady flow of electricity.

4. The electricity moves to a transformer which increases the voltage to send the current out over long distances. Before it reaches your home, the electricity moves through another transformer that decreases the voltage to make it safer for your home.

Coal

Boiler (Furnace)

Steam

Turbine

Generator

Transmission Lines

Transformer

Condenser

Water cools here

River

PLUG IT IN, TURN IT ON!

Power is delivered to your house using AC voltage. AC stands for *alternating current.* Sixty times each second, the current changes direction, from back toward the power station to flowing into your home. The change in direction happens so fast that your appliances don't notice it and the human eye cannot see it!

As electricity flows into your home all sorts of things can happen. Toasters turn electricity into heat. Lamps light living rooms. Blenders spin motors to make fruit smoothies. Electrical energy has been transformed into heat, light, and mechanical energy.

High-voltage transmission lines are the first step from the power plant to your home.

Thermal Energy:
The energy associated with heat.

When electricity passes through wire loops made of certain kinds of metal, the flow of electrons is slowed—like a traffic jam. These resistors create friction, which makes heat. Thermal energy powers:
• Toasters
• Clothes dryers
• Electric stoves

Mechanical Energy:
The energy associated with motion.

Where would we be without fans on a summer day? Sweaty! Mechanical energy also powers:
• Tiny fans in computers to keep them from over-heating.
• Hair dryers, which use both thermal and mechanical energy to blow warm air onto wet hair.
• Blenders with sharp motor-powered blades to make yummy milkshakes!

Radiant Energy:
The energy associated with light.

Flick a switch and turn on a lamp. We have bright lights at night thanks to radiant energy.
• Sunlight is a major source of radiant energy.
• Lightbulbs use electricity to create radiant energy.
• X-rays—which produce images of bones and other body parts—are an example of radiant energy.

REVIEW AND DO

Insulators
Do not conduct electricity well

Conductors
Allow the flow of electricity

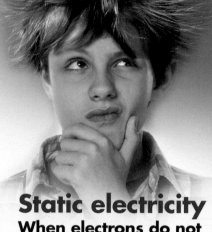

Static electricity
When electrons do not flow and build up on a material.

Electrical energy
Can be transformed into three kinds of energy

Thermal energy (heat)

Radiant energy (light)

Mechanical energy (motion)

Rules of magnetism
Opposite poles attract. Like poles repel.

Electromagnet A magnet made by passing electric current through a coil of wire wrapped around a metal core.

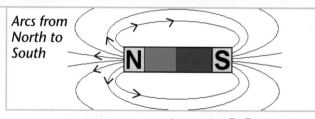

Arcs from North to South

N   S

Magnetic Field

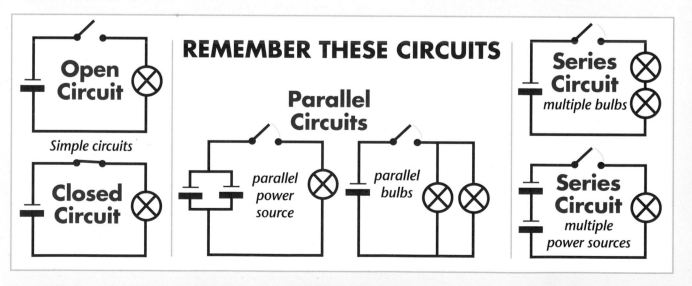

Open Circuit

Simple circuits

Closed Circuit

REMEMBER THESE CIRCUITS

Parallel Circuits

parallel power source

parallel bulbs

Series Circuit
multiple bulbs

Series Circuit
multiple power sources

Use pages 42-43 to answer question 1.

1. Describe Thomas Edison's contribution to the understanding and harnessing of electricity. What lesson can you take from his life?

Use pages 44-45 to answer questions 2 and 3.

2. Explain how static electricity is created and when it occurs in nature.
3. Describe Benjamin Franklin's contribution to the understanding of electricity.

Use pages 46-47 to answer questions 4 and 5.

4. Define the terms insulators, conductors, and circuits. List three examples of each.
5. What is the difference between an open and closed circuit?

Use pages 48-49 to answer question 6 and 7.

6. What is the difference between a parallel and series circuit?
7. Use the legend on page 48 to draw your own diagram of a functioning series circuit and a functioning parallel circuit.

Use pages 50-51 to answer question 8.

8. Draw a diagram of a magnetic field.

Use pages 52-53 to answer questions 9-11.

9. How are permanent magnets and electromagnets similar? How are they different?
10. How can you make an electromagnet?
11. Describe Michael Faraday's contribution to the understanding and harnessing of electricity.

THINK LIKE A SCIENTIST

Look around your classroom or your home and make a list of six items powered by electricity that you regularly see being used. Identify what kind or combination of energy each uses: thermal, radiant, or mechanical.

Design and draw a circuit to power a new electronic board game that has a buzzer and a light. Think about which type of circuit might work best.

DATA DETECTIVE

This line graph shows the use of electricity after Thomas Edison invented a better lightbulb that could burn for a very long time. What can you infer about the use of electricity after his invention?

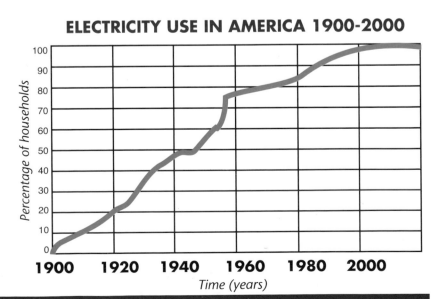

ELECTRICITY USE IN AMERICA 1900-2000

How are fruits and flowers related?

How do plants make their own food?

What is pollen?

How are spores different from seeds?

Do all plants needs insects?

Why do plants go dormant?

CHAPTER 4

LIFE PROCESSES

If there were no plants, there would be no people, birds, insects, or animals. Plants feed us and keep the Earth's environment in balance.

A fragrant rose, a prickly cactus, and a smelly onion—just some examples of the plant world's amazing diversity.

IT'S A GREEN WORLD

THE KEY TO LIFE ON EARTH

Try to picture our planet without plants. What would it be like? The land would look like the surface of the moon—barren, bleak, and lifeless. Plants are what keep us alive. Hidden inside their brightly colored petals and sweet fruits lies a secret, wonderful world.

There are close to 300,000 different kinds of plants. Some produce beautiful blossoms. Others stand over 90 meters tall or have trunks wide enough to drive a car through. Some plants smell awful, some are full of poisons, and some have powerful medicines stored in their roots and leaves that can save lives and ease pain. Many of the clothes we wear and the homes we live in are made from plants. Plants sustain our planet.

PLANTS ARE EVERYWHERE

Plants can grow in all sorts of places and thrive in a wide range of temperatures. They grow in hot deserts and in the arctic north, on rocky mountainsides and along windswept ocean dunes. What is life like for a typical plant? Let's find out.

Giant sequoias are some of the world's biggest and oldest trees.

Chandelier
Tree

A LEAFY TALE
Some trees' leaves stay green all winter. Others lose their green color, revealing red, yellow, and orange before dropping off. These trees grow new leaves when the weather warms.

FANTASTIC FRUITS
These cherimoya fruits grow mostly in South America in areas with cool temperatures.

KEY WORDS FOR PLANTS

Photosynthesis
(fow-tow-_sin_-the-sis)
The way a plant uses sunlight to convert carbon dioxide and water into sugar to use as a food source.

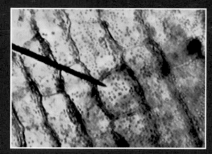

Chlorophyll
(_klor_-uh-fill)
A green chemical in plant leaves that absorbs sunlight and helps plants make sugar.

This exotic plant is called a bromeliad. The best-known member of this plant family is the pineapple.

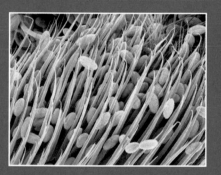

Pollen
(_pah_-lin)
Tiny grains made by a seed-bearing plant that are needed for it to reproduce.

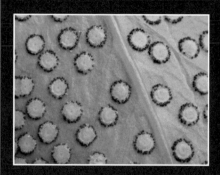

Spores
Tiny, one-celled organisms from which plants like mosses and ferns reproduce.

Every plant, from a brightly colored tulip to a smelly onion to a thorn-covered cactus, has special ways of surviving. In order for a species to survive it must have food and water. It also must be able to reproduce—to somehow make new versions of its species.

Knowing these key words will help you as you explore the amazing world of plants.

PLANT PARTS

What does the biggest tree have in common with a delicate daisy? Surprisingly, a lot!

FROM ROOT TIP TO TOP

Have you ever given someone flowers as a get-well or a thank-you? Don't forget to say "thank you" to the plants for all the hard work done by their petals, leaves, stems, and roots! Each plant part has an important job to do to help a plant thrive.

In spite of their varied appearances, many of the world's plants share the same basic structure or **anatomy** (uh-_nat_-uh-me). Even giant sequoias have things in common with a wispy weed. A tree trunk is nothing more than a _very_ thick stem.

Flowers

The often colorful part of a plant that has the things needed for the plant to reproduce.

Leaves

These thin, flat, green parts absorb sunlight and use it to help make sugar to feed the plant.

Stem

The thick part that supports the plant upright and also carries moisture and nutrients from the roots throughout the plant.

Roots

A network of teeny little "straws" that pull water and nutrients up from the soil. Roots also anchor the plant in the soil.

ROOTING FOR WATER

Even in a small plant, the roots are extensive. For example, a four-month old rye plant (a type of grass) has over 13 million tiny roots and root hairs.

EATING PLANTS: FRUIT OR VEGETABLE?

We depend on plants for much of our food, and fruits and vegetables are an important part of our diet. What is the difference between the two? A fruit is the part of a plant that contains a pit or seeds, while vegetables are cut from the stems, leaves, and roots.

Some fruits have many seeds in the edible parts—such as oranges, melons, and apples. Others have one big pit in the center, like plums or peaches. A third kind of fruit comes enclosed in a pod, such as peas and beans. Many of us think of these as vegetables but, surprisingly, they are fruits.

Carrots and potatoes are some of the most popular vegetables in America. Carrots are part of a plant's roots. Potatoes are thick plant stems that grow underground, called tubers. A stalk of asparagus is the stem of an above-ground plant, while lettuce and cabbage are leaves. Some vegetables such as broccoli and cauliflower are actually flower buds. Which is your favorite fruit or vegetable?

WHAT'S TO EAT IN THE GARDEN?
People and animals eat every part of a plant. Humans eat root vegetables, stem vegetables, leaf vegetables, and flower bulb vegetables.

TWO WAYS PLANTS REPRODUCE
Most of the world's plants fall into these two categories.

SEED-MAKERS

Flowering plants and trees reproduce by making **seeds**. *In order to make a seed, a plant needs pollen. Seeds are carried by the wind, water, or animals to other places. There, a brand-new plant can grow with the characteristics of the parent plants.*

Some seed-makers have showy bright flowers and tiny seeds. Others like big pine trees have tiny flowers and large seed pods called cones. Even grasses have teeny flowers and seeds.

SPORE-MAKERS

There is a second group of plants. They reproduce differently from seed-makers. They do not use pollen and seeds to make new versions of themselves. Instead, they have **spores**—*millions of tiny cells that allow them to self-reproduce. Under the right conditions the spores drop off, blow away, and sprout into new plants.*

FOOD POWERED BY THE SUN

How do plants make food from sunlight, water, and air?

Sunlight

The warm rays of the sun power a chemical reaction in the leaves.

THE PRODUCERS

Green plants are known as producers, because they can produce (make) their own food. That's why in supermarkets you will find fruits and vegetables in the "produce" section.

Plants produce their food through a process called **photosynthesis**. We cannot make our own food simply by standing in the sun, but we do have some surprising things in common with plants. We both take in and release gases, though we have lungs while plants have leaves. We also both have veins to carry fluids throughout our bodies. But plants have something very special that humans and other animals do *not* have—a green chemical called **chlorophyll**.

Carbon Dioxide

enters the leaves.

Oxygen

is released from the leaves into the air where animals breathe it in.

SPEAK LIKE A SCIENTIST

Photosynthesis
(fow-tow-<u>sin</u>-tha-sis)
The process in which a plant uses sunlight to convert carbon dioxide and water into sugar.

Chlorophyll
(<u>klor</u>-uh-fill)
A green chemical that helps a plant make food. It absorbs sunlight and aids the plant in making sugar.

Water and nutrients

are pulled out of the soil by the plant's root system.

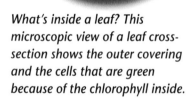

LEAF CELLS ARE FOOD FACTORIES

Leaves are the primary food-producing parts of a plant. Within leaves a special chemical reaction occurs that makes **sugar**. Sugar is a plant's food, and it provides energy for the plant, helping it grow. Plants make a lot of extra sugar and store it for later in their leaves, stems, fruits, and roots. That's good news for the animals that eat plants! Next time you eat broccoli or potatoes, say thanks to the plant!

FOOD FROM THE AIR?

When you think of making food, you might think of putting a few slices of cheese on some bread. Plants do something entirely different. They turn air into food. One of the gasses found in air is carbon dioxide. In the leaf, chlorophyll uses sunlight to combine carbon dioxide and water into sugar. Chlorophyll gives leaves their green color.

We have lungs that inhale oxygen and exhale carbon dioxide. Plants don't have lungs, but their leaves allow carbon dioxide in and oxygen out. To put it simply, humans and plants take in and release the opposite gases. A lot of people think that plants make oxygen for us. They don't. They just happen to make a lot of extra oxygen while making sugar. Plants actually use oxygen when they need to use their sugar supplies to help them grow.

What's inside a leaf? This microscopic view of a leaf cross-section shows the outer covering and the cells that are green because of the chlorophyll inside.

HANDS-ON SCIENCE

PLANT PARTY!

Does the amount of light affect photosynthesis?

1. Choose three plants of the same size and type. Measure and record their height and leaf sizes. Water all three with an identical amount of water.

2. Place one plant on a sunny windowsill.

3. Place the second plant in a shady spot out of the sunlight.

4. Cover the third plant with a large brown paper bag. Poke a few tiny holes in it with a pencil point so the plant gets some air.

5. After one week, graph the growth results and record any qualitative data.

Does the amount of water affect photosynthesis?

1. Start with three identical plants of equal size and type. Place them on a sunny windowsill.

2. Water one with 50 ml of water every other day.

3. Water one with 50 ml of water every five days.

4. Do not water the third plant.

5. After two weeks, graph the growth results. Which plant grew the most?

Based on your two experiments, what can you determine about the roles of sunlight and water in plant growth?

PARTS OF A FLOWER

HOW SOME PLANTS MAKE NEW PLANTS

Like all life, plants must be able to reproduce for their species to continue. In many plants, the flower does this job. The flower produces seeds that hold the materials needed to create new plants. The key players on the seed-making team are the **stigma** (_stig_-mah), the **pistil** (_pist_-ul), the **stamen** (_stay_-min), and little, sticky specks called **pollen** (_pah_-lin).

Flowers have many colors, shapes, and fragrances. All that beauty has a purpose. It attracts insects! Many plants depend on insects—especially bees and butterflies— to help them spread pollen. Some birds, bats, and mammals help too. When pollen reaches a flower ovary, a baby plant **embryo** (_em_-bree-oh) is formed. A seed develops around the embryo to nourish and protect it until it is ready to grow into a new plant.

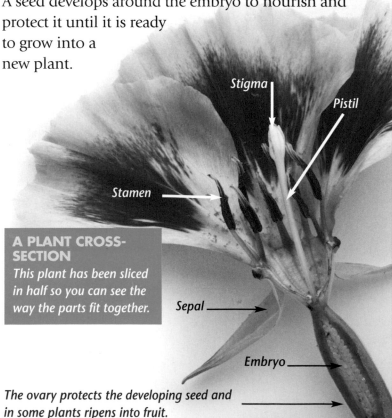

A PLANT CROSS-SECTION
This plant has been sliced in half so you can see the way the parts fit together.

Stigma

Pistil

Stamen

Sepal

Embryo

The ovary protects the developing seed and in some plants ripens into fruit.

Stigma
The sticky tip at the top of the pistil that receives the pollen.

Pistil
The stalk in the center of a flower down which the pollen travels.

Stamen
The parts that surround the pistil. They are covered with pollen.

The ovary

Embryo
The baby plant that starts as a single cell within a seed.

Seed
A "package" containing the plant embryo and some stored food, surrounded by a cover called the seed coat.

Sepal
The part under the flower that protects the flower as it develops.

SPEAK LIKE A SCIENTIST
....
Pollen
(_pah-lin_)
A tiny grain-like substance that combines with the ovule to start the process of seed-making in many plants.

Don't swat that bee! It might be in the middle of helping to make a new plant!

POLLINATION
THE BIRDS AND THE BEES

Look carefully at the bee on this page. Does it have yellow dandruff? Of course not! It is covered with **pollen**.

Pollen is one of the most important ingredients in the making of a new plant. Seeds are produced by the union of ovary cells (stored inside the ovary) and pollen cells. As pollen reaches an ovule, the two fuse to form an embryo that will develop into a seed. But how does pollen get inside the plant?

Although birds, butterflies, and other animals can carry pollen, the best little pollinator out there is the bee. Bees are perfectly designed to be pollen carriers. They have hairy bodies that attract the sticky pollen. As bees buzz from flower to flower, they collect a sugary nectar cupped in the flowers.

While nose-diving deep into each flower, the pollen grains rub off onto the bee. When the bee flies into a new flower, the pollen gets caught on the sticky stigma. There the pollen starts its trip down to the ovary where it begins the process of making a new plant.

Not all plants are pollinated by insects. Grass and tree pollens travel with the wind and some aquatic plants rely on water to carry pollen. But no matter how it gets there, pollen is the key to making a new plant.

Pollen gets caught on the stigma, then travels down the pistil.

Each pollen grain then sends out a thin tube that reaches down to pierce the ovary. An embryo is formed.

In order for a seed to develop, a plant needs pollen.

Ovary

ALLERGY ALERT
Some folks are very sensitive to pollen floating in the air and suffer from allergies. Sneezes eject the pollen from your nose.

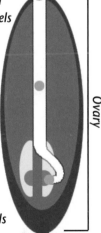

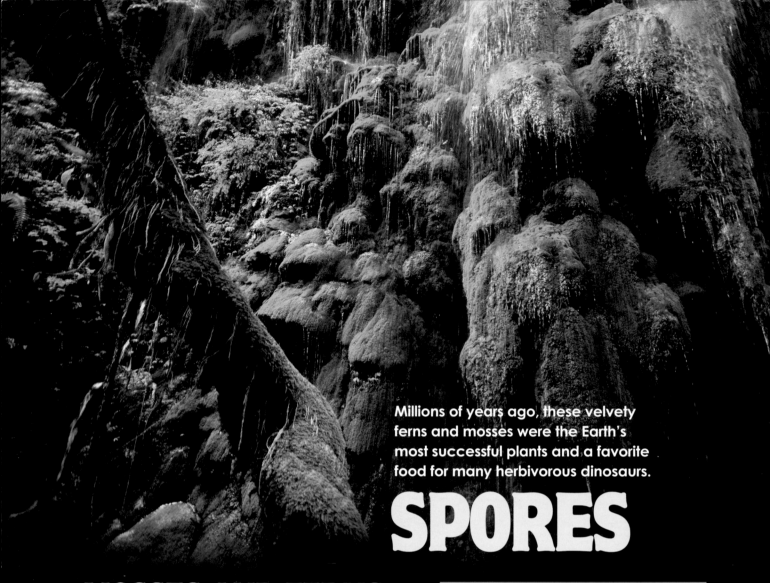

Millions of years ago, these velvety ferns and mosses were the Earth's most successful plants and a favorite food for many herbivorous dinosaurs.

SPORES

MOSSES AND FERNS

Walk into a damp, cool, shady place and you might notice something green and fuzzy covering many of the rocks. It grows very low to the ground and looks a bit like green carpet. What is it? Meet **moss**—a kind of plant that is very different from the leafy, flowering plants you have just learned about. What makes it different?

Mosses do not have seeds or flowers. Instead, they have **spores**. Unlike a seed which is made by pollination, a spore has everything it needs to reproduce itself. All by itself, a spore can grow into a completely new plant. Mosses are not the only plants that reproduce by spores.

Ferns have lots of feathery leaves, called **fronds**. Unlike the short mosses, ferns can grow to be quite tall. But like mosses, ferns have no seeds or flowers. They also reproduce by releasing spores that are then carried away by the wind to other areas.

SPEAK LIKE A SCIENTIST

Spore

A microscopic, one-celled organism from which some bacteria, fungi, and certain green plants reproduce.

Spores are transported by wind and water or in the waste products of animals, such as moose or reindeer, that have eaten moss or ferns.

A microscopic view of a moss spore

A velvety moss plant

MIGHTY MOSSES
Mosses
Small, furry plants that grow in close clumps in damp, shady locations. They do not have flowers or seeds,

They may be small—usually never taller than an inch or two—but mosses are a vital part of our ecosystem. There are about 24,000 different kinds of mosses, and they can be found growing on rocks and tree trunks as well as in the soil. Mosses have been around for about 280 million years—much longer than ferns.

FEATHERY FERNS

Ferns love the damp and shaded areas of forests, ravines, and gorges. That is where you will most likely find these ancient plants.

Early in the spring, a single stalk that looks a bit like a violin neck will emerge. Slowly, it will uncurl and the fronds will spread.

Two hundred million years ago, much of the Earth was covered with fern forests, and ferns were the most abundant plant on the planet. Plant-eating dinosaurs thrived on a diet of ferns. Today, there are still about 12,000 different kinds of fern.

Ferns
Plants with feather-like fronds and no flowers or seeds. Like mosses, ferns reproduce with spores.

FERN-FAVORITES!
Large plant-eating dinosaurs like the Apatosaurus feasted on ferns.

A feathery fern

FERN SPORES
The underside of the fern frond holds clumps of spores.

LINK TO THE PAST

Today many parts of Virginia have rich coal deposits, but millions of years ago, those areas were covered with vast fern forests. As ferns died and decayed, the layers were compressed over time. Intense pressure led to a buildup of heat, and the result was a hardened lump—coal. Today it is not uncommon to find fossilized imprints of ancient ferns in a hunk of coal.

Swamp

Decaying plants

Heat

Coal

Can you spot the fossilized fern prints in this lump of coal?

....

Dormancy

(*door*-mun-see)

A period when life functions are slowed or suspended—brought on by changes in the environment.

When winter comes you can pull on warm clothes. A bear can curl up in a sheltered den. A plant cannot, so it must come up with a way to survive extremes in temperature.

DORMANCY

SEASONS OF LIFE

Put a head of lettuce in the freezer for a few hours. Take it out and let it thaw. What will happen? You will end up with a soggy, oozing, slimy mess. As the water freezes and expands, the plant's cell walls burst. Lettuce cannot survive in the cold.

Other plants have developed ways to survive the bitter cold—**dormancy**. The cycle of the seasons is a perfect way to see how they do this.

Changing Leaves

Why do leaves change color in autumn? You know that chlorophyll gives plants their green color, but leaves have other colors too, hidden by the green pigment. Some plants have pigments like the ones that make corn yellow and carrots orange. As the weather cools, leaves produce a third pigment—the one that makes cranberries and cherries red. When chlorophyll production stops in the autumn, the other colors can finally be seen in all their bright beauty.

FROM SPRING TO SPRING

Think about the seasons in Virgina. Let's start with springtime. The days start to grow longer. The sun is brighter. It rains a lot and there is plenty of moisture. Sunlight and water are two important ingredients for photosynthesis, so new growth appears on plants and trees. Summer brings long days with lots of sunlight. Plants and trees are at the peak of their growth at this point. By late summer, the growing slows, then stops.

The days are growing shorter and there is less sunlight, so the plants and trees begin to store food and energy within their roots, stems or trunks, and branches. The tree lets its leaves dry out and fall off as the plant hoards sugar to survive winter's cold. By November, many plants and trees look like they are dead—leafless and brittle. But they are not. They are simply **dormant**—waiting for those first warm licks of sunlight and spring's lengthening days to wake up and begin growing again.

EVERGREENS

Why do some trees lose their leaves every fall, while others manage to survive with their greenery intact? Some plants, such as fir and pine trees and holly bushes, have tougher leaves or needles. They have less water in their cells and a waxy coating to protect them when a freeze occurs. Even though they too have stopped growing and are also dormant during the winter, their thicker, tougher needles or leaves can withstand the cold. Because they remain green all year, they are called evergreens—a perfect name to describe them.

ADAPTING TO MOISTURE AND LIGHT

Bitter cold is not the only reason a plant might go dormant. Some desert plants survive the driest periods of the year by doing the same thing a tree in a cold climate might do. Other plants have a very short blooming season, then quickly fall into dormancy until the next seasonal rainy period arrives.

All plants need light and moisture. Many plants have developed ways to adapt to difficult growing conditions besides becoming dormant. On the forest floor of thick rainforests there is very little sunlight, and yet plants also grow there. A cactus can survive very nicely with only a small amount of rain a year. Some plants will only bloom after the sun sets, and their blossoms will close by dawn. The plant world's ability to adapt to difficult conditions is truly amazing.

PINECONES AND HOLLY BERRIES

Both hold seeds! Pinecones are clusters of seeds in seed pods. Bright red holly berries hold seeds inside.

LINK TO THE PAST

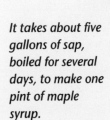

It takes about five gallons of sap, boiled for several days, to make one pint of maple syrup.

The American Indians knew that in early spring, a certain type of maple tree produces a sweet liquid. As the trees wake from their winter sleep, the sugar they stored deep within is carried up in water from the roots to the leaves. This is called sap. The American Indians drilled little holes into the trunks to tap the sap. Drip by drip, the Indians filled pots with the sticky liquid, then boiled off the watery part. When colonists from Europe arrived in North America, they learned the secret of the maple tree in early spring. For many years, maple syrup was the only sweetener in the colonies.

REVIEW AND DO

Parts of a common plant

- Flower
- Stem
- Leaf
- Root

Photosynthesis

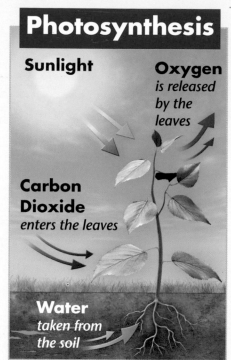

- Sunlight
- **Oxygen** *is released by the leaves*
- **Carbon Dioxide** *enters the leaves*
- **Water** *taken from the soil*

Chlorophyll

A green chemical in a plant that uses sunlight to combine carbon dioxide and water into sugar.

- Stigma
- Stamen
- Pistil
- Sepal
- Seeds
- Embryo

Remember these parts for plant reproduction

Pollen sticks to the stigma and then travels down through the pistil to the ovary. The pollen and ovary cells fuse to form embryos that develop into seeds.

Bees are excellent pollen carriers.

Ferns and Mosses

Plants that reproduce with spores rather than seeds.

Dormancy

A period when life functions are slowed or suspended—brought on by changes in the environment.

Use pages 62-63 to answer questions 1 and 2.

1. Draw a picture of a plant and label the roots, stem, leaves, and flowers. Next to each label, briefly explain the function of each plant part.

2. What are the two different ways plants reproduce? How are they similar? How are they different?

Use pages 64-65 to answer question 3.

3. Use the words in the box below to write a paragraph explaining the process of photosynthesis.

sunlight • chlorophyll • water • carbon dioxide • oxygen • sugar

Use pages 66-67 to answer question 4.

4. Create a diagram illustrating the reproductive process (pollination) using arrows and labels. You must use the following words in your diagram: stamen, stigma, pistil, sepal, embryo, pollen, and seed.

Use pages 68-69 to answer question 5.

5. How do ferns and mosses reproduce?

Use pages 70-71 to answer questions 6 and 7.

6. Why do plants become dormant?

7. How do dormant plants respond to light? How do they respond to moisture?

THINK LIKE A SCIENTIST

Take a walk outside and look for different kinds of plants and trees. Make a list or a drawing of each plant and decide if the plant reproduces using seeds or spores. Which type of reproduction occurs more often in the plants you found? What can you infer about the plants in your area?

DATA DETECTIVE

In the United States, honey bees pollinate up to 30% of the food Americans eat. Some of these foods are oranges, cucumbers, grapes, and apples. Based on the population trend of honey bees, what can you infer the impact will be on the growth of these fruits?

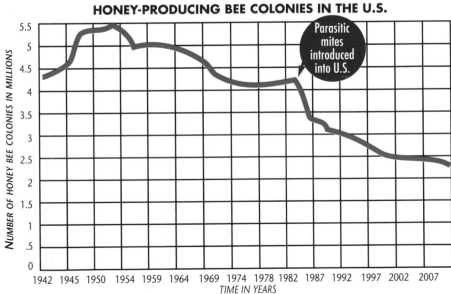

HONEY-PRODUCING BEE COLONIES IN THE U.S.

Parasitic mites introduced into U.S.

NUMBER OF HONEY BEE COLONIES IN MILLIONS

TIME IN YEARS

Why do elephants have trunks?

How do geese know it is time to migrate?

What is a food web?

How does the sun affect how and where we live?

74

CHAPTER 5

LIVING SYSTEMS

Long beaks. Webbed feet. Sharp tusks. Blubber. Hibernating. Migrating. Just a few adaptations that help organisms survive and thrive.

Perfect for paddling! A duck has a beak that can scoop up pond plants, feathers that make it easier to float, and those magnificent flippered feet.

SURVIVAL OF THE FITTEST
THE DRIVE TO SURVIVE

Picture a duck without webbed feet or a giraffe with a short stubby neck. Imagine a bright red lion trying to hide in the tall brown grasses of the African savannah. All creatures are constantly adapting to the world in which they live. This is sometimes a very slow, very long process that takes hundreds of thousands of years. Other times it can happen in only a couple of generations. The ways we change in order to survive are called **adaptations** (*ah-dap-tay-shunz*). Some adaptations are physical—thicker fur, bigger ears, night vision. Others are behavioral—knowing which berries taste yummiest, or when the weather will grow cold and it will be best to move to a warm place.

Think about what *you* need to survive. You must have food, water, and shelter. Add to those what our entire species—humankind—must do to survive. We need to create new generations of humans and have *them* survive. These are our basic **life's needs**. All species, from a microscopic bacteria to a massive blue whale, have the exact same needs.

SHARING THE PLANET

All of the diverse organisms of the world rely on Earth's resources. The loss of one type of organism, due to disease or a destroyed habitat, can be devastating for the other species around it. Survival is a never-ending challenge for all of the world's creatures. Here's how some do it!

A VERY LONG ADAPTATION
Over generations, giraffes evolved longer and longer necks, which made them better able to reach high, leafy tree branches that other animals could not reach. They had a food source all to themselves.

Structural Adaptation

Physical attributes that help living things obtain food, survive harsh weather, and meet life's needs.

Behavioral Adaptation

Activities that living things do to meet life's needs, such as migrating or developing hunting skills.

Community
(kuh-mew-nit-ee)

A group of different organisms that share the same region. They depend on and interact with one another.

Niche
(neesh)

The role played by a species in the community it inhabits: where it lives, what it eats, and what preys on it.

Ecosystem
(ee-koh-sis-tum)

All the populations of living organisms and nonliving things—water, rocks, and soil—that interact with one another in a certain place.

This tree frog lives in a rainforest ecosystem in Brazil. It has several adaptations such as sticky feet and a leafy color that help it survive.

Big ears—all the better to hear with. Big eyes—all the better to see with. Big teeth—all the better to eat with. These are all…

STRUCTURAL ADAPTATIONS

BETTER ABLE TO...

You do NOT want to get your finger in the way of a toucan's razor sharp beak. That bright bill is a brilliant **structural adaptation** that helps these rainforest-dwellers survive. The toucan's long, lightweight, curved beak is made from keratin—the same material as human fingernails. The length and sharpness allows the bird to reach berries tucked deep within a jungle plant's dense foliage and pluck them off. It also regulates the bird's body temperature. That beak has helped the toucan live successfully in its environment.

Organisms that are best able to find or make food grow bigger and stronger. A plant with sharp thorns that protects its tender young leaves from being eaten, thrives. A skunk with smelly "stink" glands can keep predators away. Any living thing that adapts to the conditions where it lives—be it rainforests, deserts, or icy wastelands—has a big advantage. We call this "survival of the fittest" because being "fit" means that the organism is healthy and therefore will survive and reproduce.

WAYS TO ADAPT PHYSICALLY

An insect that looks like a plant

A frog that looks like a rock

CAMOUFLAGE

Creatures that can hide themselves from their predators have a greater chance of surviving. They do this by looking like their surroundings so they become difficult to see.

A large owl

A small butterfly

MIMICRY

Physical attributes that make an animal look bigger, or more dangerous, can keep them safe. A predator might confuse the fragile butterfly's fake "eyes" with those of a large owl.

HIT THE HORNS
Some males use horns to fight and attract a mate. The bigger the horns, the better.

SPEAK LIKE A SCIENTIST
....
Structural Adaptation
(*struck-chur-ul* • *ah-dap-**tay**-shun*)
Physical attributes that help organisms meet life's needs. These include: fur, sharp teeth, night vision, whiskers, thick shells, hooves, venom, and more.

Thumbs are a useful adaptation. Animals with thumbs could grasp things more easily which helped them survive.

CHANGE IS GOOD

Look at the gibbon on the right. Millions of years ago, its ancestors had a different type of hand with closely attached fingers. One day, one of those ancestral moms gave birth to babies that had slightly more separated thumbs. Those special thumbs allowed her babies to grab more firmly onto trees. They traveled faster, could gather more food, and grew bigger and stronger. They grew up and had babies of their own. The luckiest of those babies had even more highly separated thumbs. They passed this superior physical trait on to their babies and in time, most gibbons had the amazing thumb. Structural adaptations are a huge factor in helping a species survive, but it takes more than that to succeed. You have to use your brain too. Read more on the next page!

PLANTS ADAPT TOO

A furry flower from icy Switzerland.

Animals are not the only organisms that develop adaptations. Plants also adapt. Would you want to eat a mouthful of thorns? A prickly desert cactus has all those sharp spines to keep predators away. Some rainforest plants have developed huge leaves to help collect limited sunlight under the dense, thick forest canopy. Many meadow grasses have developed seeds that will easily blow away in a light wind to help the plants reproduce. In freezing climates, plants have developed furry, wax-like coatings that help them resist cold and wind, and right here in Virginia, dormancy helps certain plants survive our chilly winters.

There is a saying that a leopard cannot change its spots. But it sure can change its mind!

BEHAVIORAL ADAPTATION

LEARNING TO LIVE

You just read about how an animal or plant *looks*. Now learn about how an animal *acts*. **Behavioral adaptations** play a big role in helping an animal survive. These are all the things an organism *does* to find food and protect its young.

Some behaviors are learned by watching an adult, or through a repeated experience. Other behaviors are instinctive—something a critter knows how to do from the moment it is born—such as spiders who know how to spin a web and babies who know how to suck thumbs.

ADAPTING BY DOING

INSTINCT

Behavior an animal is born with and does not need to be taught.

MIGRATION

Moving from one region to another and then back again to avoid difficult weather, to find more food, or to raise babies more safely.

SAFETY IN NUMBERS

One of the most important behaviors involves whether or not to live in a group. Many animals live in herds, flocks, or gaggles. Small fish stay in "schools" because from far away, they look like one enormous fish. This protects them from being eaten by larger underwater predators. Cattle, too, like to stay close together for protection from wily coyotes and wild wolves.

Primates, such as monkeys and baboons, have large social circles. They groom one another, warn each other of danger, and scheme to become "popular."

HAPPY HUNTING
This bear cub has learned the best way to snag a salmon.

COMPARING ADAPTATIONS

Here are some examples of the difference between a penguin's structural and behavioral adaptations.

HOW THEY LOOK

- **Black backs, white tummies:** Black absorbs the sun's heat, which helps penguins stay warm in their cold climate. While diving for food, a penguin's white belly helps it hide from underwater predators and prey swimming below, by blending with the bright sky.

- **Blubber:** A thick layer of fat helps retain body heat.

- **Feathers:** Densely packed, each has a special air pocket that helps trap heat.

Can you see how closely these pin-like feathers are packed?

HOW THEY ACT

- **Huddling in groups:** They stay in closely-packed groups to protect themselves both from the cold and from predators.

- **Diving with weights:** They sometimes dive for food with a rock tucked in a special pouch in their throats. This makes them heavier and keeps them from floating to the surface too quickly.

- **Nest-building:** Some types of penguin build simple nests with rocks.

THE SCHOOL OF MOM AND DAD

Just as you learn by watching the grown-ups around you, so do other animals. Young bears learn the best fishing spots and how to wait patiently for the best moment to pounce. Otters have to be taught how to swim. Baby egrets learn that if they stand quietly in the water with their wings outstretched, their shadows will attract fish.

Young chimps learn to make termite-hunting sticks by watching the grown-ups strip and sharpen a twig and then use it to collect some tasty termites nestled deep inside rotting logs.

The same skills that you depend on to learn—memory, trial and error, and repeated practice—are the same things that many animals also do.

PRETENDING TO BE DEAD
Some behaviors help protect animals from harm. Opossums sometimes "play dead." They will roll over, become stiff, and almost stop breathing. The animal that was hunting it will think it is dead and move on.

COMMUNITIES

You live in a community in Virginia, but all across our vast planet there are millions of communities—groups of organisms who depend on one another to survive.

NATURE'S VILLAGES

When you think about your **community**, you might think of your school, shopping mall, fire station, and library. But there are communities in nature as well. An ocean reef community is very different from a grasslands community. A marsh community in the Chesapeake Bay supports totally different life forms from a desert community. But all these communities have one big thing in common: they depend on energy from the sun, which plants have stored as sugar. Plants are the base of the food web for all the organisms that live in that community.

IN THE NEIGHBORHOOD

Every large community has smaller communities. For example, a forest community might have a pine forest neighborhood. A tidal marsh community could include a seagrass-bed neighborhood. Each of these smaller areas has a very specific group of creatures and plants that lives and interacts in them. Each of these habitats is unique.

Along the ocean's shores the air is salty and the soil is sandy. Many plants cannot grow near salty water, but beach grasses thrive in the salty air. Shellfish, such as crabs, that burrow in the sand and live off sea plants and smaller shellfish, could never survive on top of a mountain in the Blue Ridge. Marshes like the Great Dismal Swamp are the perfect place for the frogs and toads that would die in a dry desert.

WON'T YOU BE MY NEIGHBOR?

Think of an apartment building. That building is filled with a **population** of people—a group of the same organisms living in the same place. But there are many other species sharing the community with them. There are bugs and birds, dogs and cats and maybe a few mice—many different populations living side by side. Populations only survive because they are well adapted to their **ecosystem**. What is an ecosystem? It is all the populations plus the nonliving things—waterways, rocks, and soil—that interact with each other in a certain place.

SPEAK LIKE A SCIENTIST

Community
(kuh-_mew_-nit-ee)
Different organisms that live together in a particular physical environment.

Population
(pop-you-_lay_-shun)
A group of organisms of the same kind living in the same place.

These geese are a population.

They share a community with other living things.

Their community is part of an ecosystem

THREE VIRGINIA COMMUNITIES

Ecosystem	Plant Life	Animal Life

Atlantic Ocean: Shoreline

Beach Grass

Algae

Blue Crabs

Clams

Gulls

The Great Dismal Swamp: Marshes

Bald Cypress

Ferns

Otters

Frogs

Blue Ridge: Mountains

Dogwood Trees

Black-eyed Susans

Black Bears

White-tailed Deer

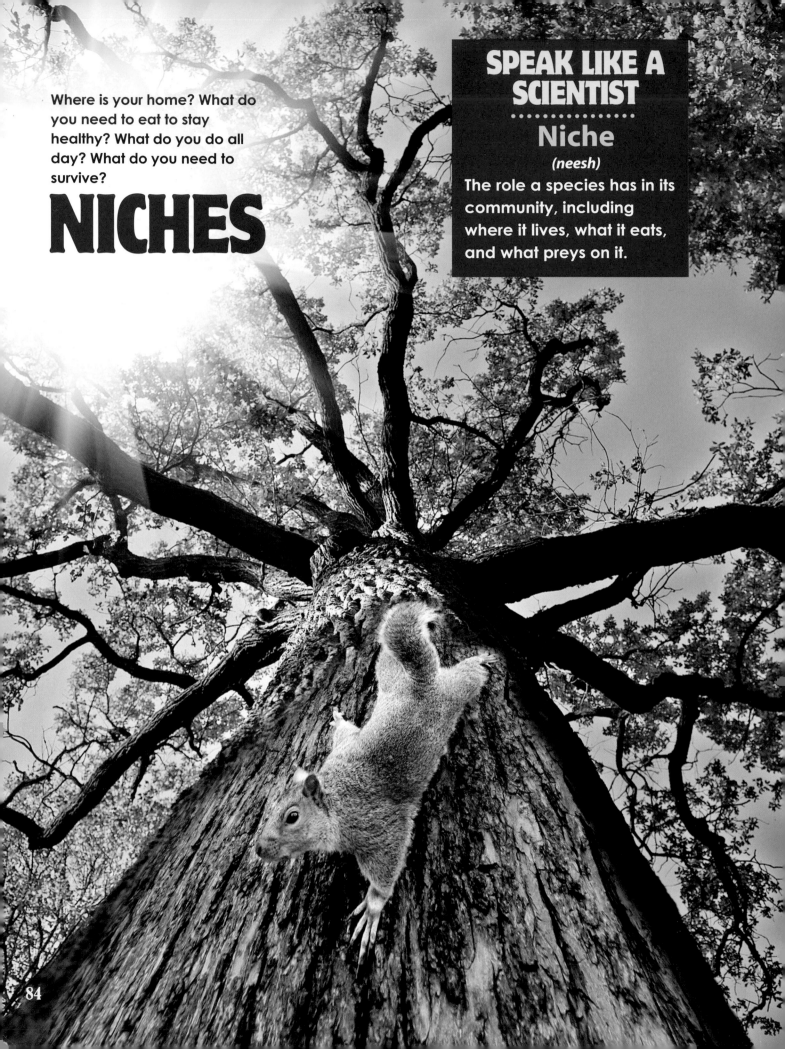

Where is your home? What do you need to eat to stay healthy? What do you do all day? What do you need to survive?

NICHES

84

DO YOU HAVE A NICHE?

You live in a specific place in Virginia. You might like to eat fruits, veggies, ice cream, and peanut butter sandwiches. Luckily you're at the top of the food chain, so nothing eats you (although plenty of bacteria love to live on and *in* you). You go to school and pitch in at home with chores. You need food, water, shelter, and friends. That's your **niche**. Every living thing, even a slimy maggot, has a niche. Let's think about a blueberry bush's niche.

- It often lives on mountain slopes.
- It needs a place to grow that has water, sunlight, and good soil.
- It needs pollinators, like bees, to bring pollen to its flowers so that it can make seeds and reproduce. Its flowers provide nectar to attract those pollinators.
- It needs a way to disperse its seeds so it makes berries to hold the seeds. These are eaten by hungry bears, birds, mice, and skunks that then wander off and deposit the seeds in their droppings.
- It has branches that provide a safe haven from predators for small animals and birds.
- It has tasty leaves that deer, insects, and rabbits nibble on. As long as they don't eat too many, the plant can survive too.

This is the blueberry bush's niche. It is the role it plays in its community. No two types of organisms occupy exactly the same niche in a community. When thinking of niches think:

> **1. Where does it live? 2. What does it eat?**
> **3. What eats it? 4. What does it do?**
> **5. What does it need?**

AN EMPTY NICHE

If all blueberry bushes in a particular area fall over and die, it is a problem for the community. The small animals that find shelter in its branches will have to find new homes. The bears and birds won't have an important food source. Every community has many niches, and they are linked together.

Sadly, species die out, or are damaged by a natural disaster such as a forest fire, or are driven away by humans who want to build parking lots. An empty niche can affect the entire community. Sometimes it is a disaster, but sometimes it can help another creature thrive. For example, when the dinosaurs died out, mammals flourished.

What's My Niche?
Each of these animals or plants has a role to play. What are their niches?

BEAVER

My niche is: *Swamp dweller, dam builder, and tree cutter. I eat bark, aquatic plants, roots, and grasses. Bears and coyotes eat me. I build dams and houses made of twigs for a safe place to live and raise my babies.*

CARDINAL

My niche is: *Nest-builder in dense shrubby areas along the edges of forests. I am an eater of flower buds and insects. I am a spreader of seeds. I am a source of food for owls, hawks, snakes, raccoons, and red foxes.*

SUNFLOWER

My niche is: *Producer of seeds and oils. I produce my own food using photosynthesis. I am a member of the meadow community and am eaten by squirrels, chipmunks, and humans.*

This fisherman is a part of the cycle of life in the Chesapeake. Notice the birds circling overhead hoping to snag a fish or two!

CYCLES OF LIFE

The Chesapeake Bay is home to many different communities. Many of these communities form a cycle like the one shown below.

Birth. Growth. Death. Everything that lives has a cycle, and every living thing has the ability to create new life. Even more amazing is the way living things interact with one another in order to survive.

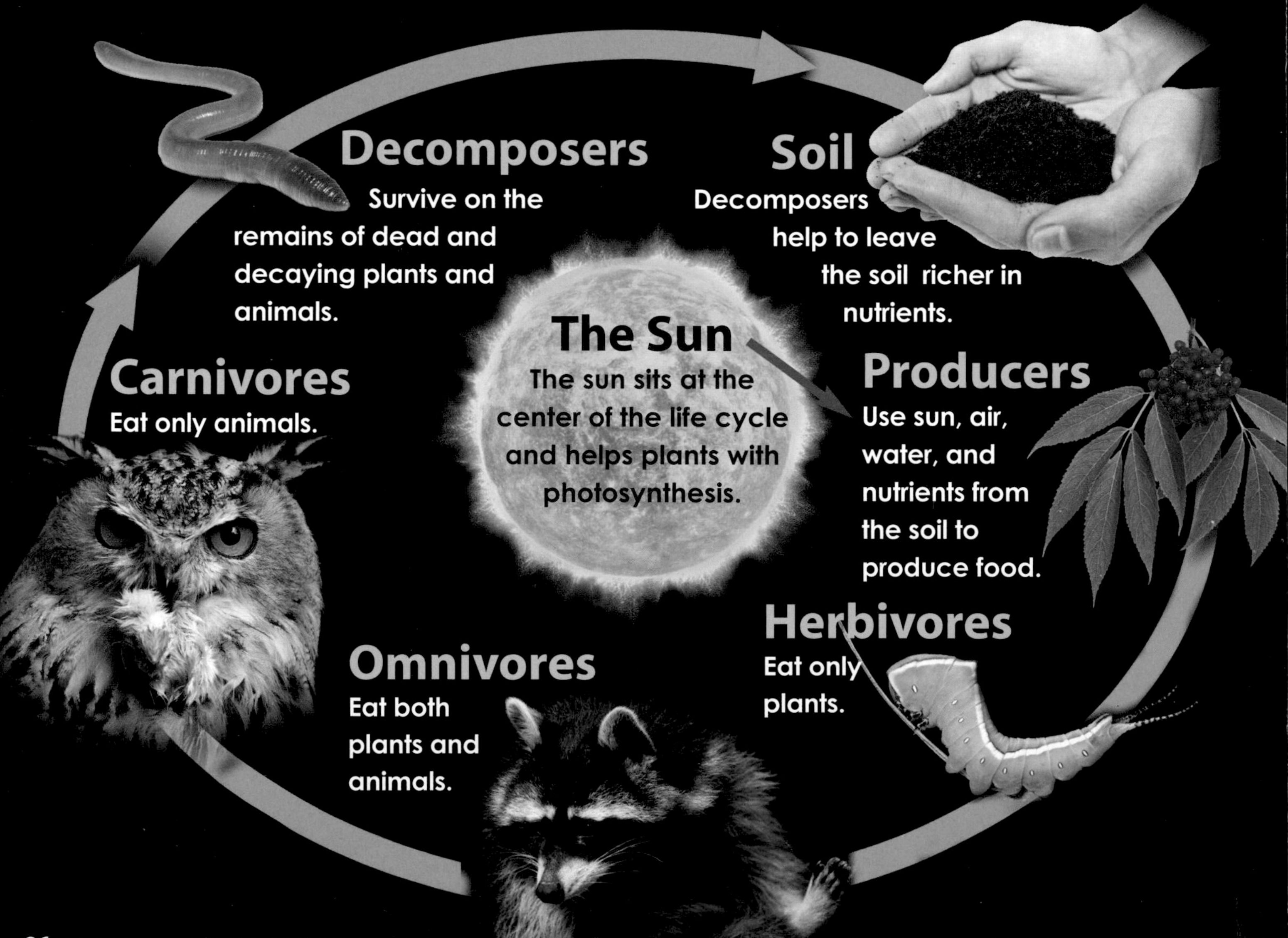

Decomposers
Survive on the remains of dead and decaying plants and animals.

Soil
Decomposers help to leave the soil richer in nutrients.

The Sun
The sun sits at the center of the life cycle and helps plants with photosynthesis.

Producers
Use sun, air, water, and nutrients from the soil to produce food.

Carnivores
Eat only animals.

Herbivores
Eat only plants.

Omnivores
Eat both plants and animals.

TWO SPECIES AND THEIR LIFE CYCLES

1. An adult butterfly lays many eggs.

2. The eggs hatch. The caterpillars grow. This is the larva stage.

Every living thing changes during its life cycle, but some creatures change more than others!

BUTTERFLIES: LAND AND AIR

An earthbound caterpillar and a lofty monarch butterfly.

3. They spin a chrysalis.

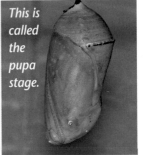

This is called the pupa stage.

Life for colorful butterflies begins as a clump of teeny eggs, each not much bigger than this period. For several weeks they will live as earth-dwellers, crawling around and eating leaves all day, but soon they will undergo a huge change. Each caterpillar will form a chrysalis in which it will slowly transform into a butterfly. When the butterfly emerges it will be able to fly! Its niche has totally changed. The butterfly now drinks nectar from plants instead of munching on leaves. Instead of crawling on the ground it now flies great distances.

4. Inside the chrysalis big changes take place.

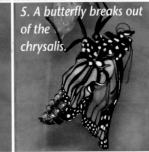

5. A butterfly breaks out of the chrysalis.

2. The tadpoles hatch from eggs.

1. A female frog lays thousands of eggs in water.

They use gills to breathe.

3. Limbs develop. Soon the tadpole will begin to breathe air.

4. The frog finally sheds its tadpole tail.

FROGS: WATER AND LAND

Wade through a pond on a warm spring day and you may see hundreds of little sacs that look a bit like eyeballs. These are frogs' eggs. Over the next few weeks, they will hatch into squirming tadpoles. After a few more weeks, the tadpoles will develop hind limbs and finally forelimbs. At that point, the frog will be able to leave underwater life behind and climb ashore to start its life as an adult frog. Where once this bullfrog swam like a fish and used gills to breathe, it now leaps and lounges at the water's edge. Quite a difference!

Not all living things have such widely changing life cycles as a frog and butterfly, but all living things must learn how to survive at each stage of life's journey.

This frog has changed from a fish-like creature with gills to a land-dweller with lungs.

Draw an arrow from an organism to what eats it, and you will soon have a web as complex as a spider's.

A VIRGINIA FOOD WEB

These arrows show how energy flows from one organism to the next. It looks very complicated because it is!

Hawks

Coyotes

Fish

Birds

Frogs
Eat plants as tadpoles, but become carnivores as adults.

Ducks

LINK TO THE PAST
The Virginia Indians
This food web shows how some of Virginia's first peoples lived off the land. They were at the top of the food chain and dined on omnivores, herbivores, and plants. They also put the "leftovers" to good use for other life's needs. Animal skins, shells, and grasses were useful for clothing, defense, and shelter.

Deer

HERBIVORES
These creatures eat only plants. Some are large mammals, some are high-flying bees and butterflies, and some are sea dwellers.

Berries

PRODUCERS
Plant parts provide energy for every ecosystem. Without them there would be no herbivores, omnivores, or carnivores.

Flowers

Grasses

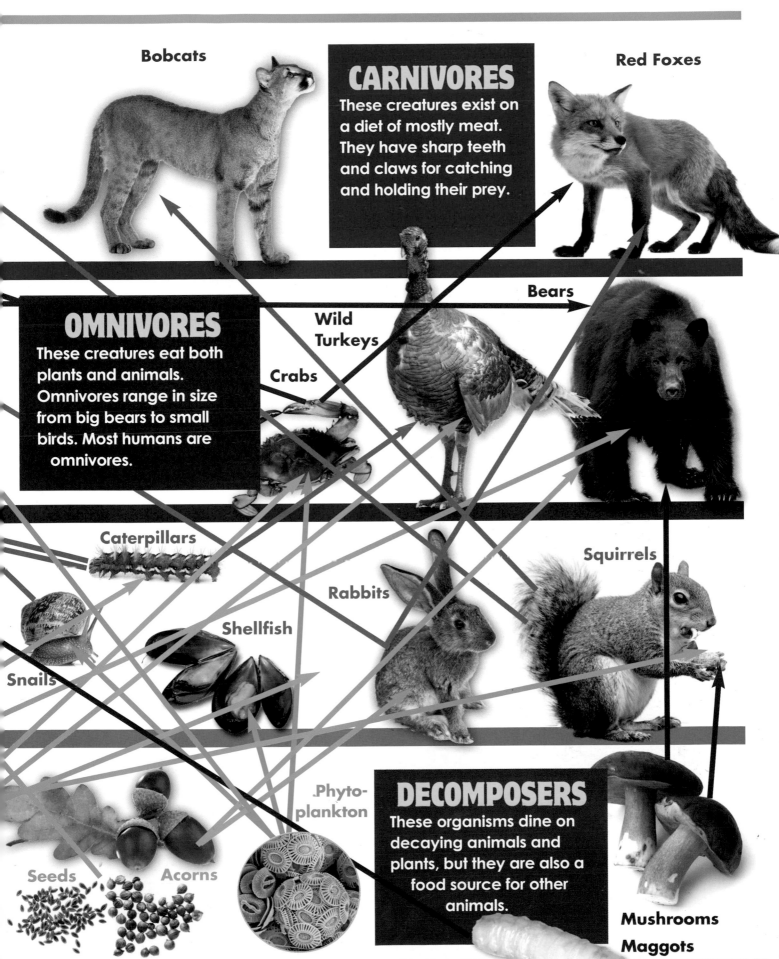

Bobcats

Red Foxes

CARNIVORES
These creatures exist on a diet of mostly meat. They have sharp teeth and claws for catching and holding their prey.

Bears

Wild Turkeys

OMNIVORES
These creatures eat both plants and animals. Omnivores range in size from big bears to small birds. Most humans are omnivores.

Crabs

Caterpillars

Squirrels

Rabbits

Shellfish

Snails

Phyto-plankton

DECOMPOSERS
These organisms dine on decaying animals and plants, but they are also a food source for other animals.

Seeds

Acorns

Mushrooms

Maggots

(teeny underwater plants)

HUMANS AND THE ECOSYSTEM

People have left very big marks on the Earth. Some are positive. Others are negative. What big mark will <u>you</u> leave?

CROP DUSTING
Some say it's harmful. Other's say it's good. But there can be no doubt that problems can occur when pesticide spray drifts onto homes or seeps into the water supply.

A DIFFICULT PROBLEM

Imagine that you are a farmer. You wake up one morning, walk out to your fields, and discover that insects have devoured a large section of your crops. You are pretty upset, and it is very tempting to think about spraying a **pesticide** (*pest-uh-side*) to kill the insects on the parts of your crops that have not yet been eaten.

If there is widespread damage to crops, there will not be enough food. But what if those hungry beetles, borers, or hornworms are all destroyed? What happens to the environment?

Some beetles can be extremely destructive. But other beetles, like ladybugs, are very helpful to farmers.

TO SPRAY OR NOT TO SPRAY

All of the Earth's species are busy fighting for their space. We humans are very smart and many times we think we have figured out a way to defeat a pest. But it's not that easy. Wipe out a particular kind of bug, and it will change the community in which those bugs lived. Those bugs are a food source for many other species. But suppose all pesticides were banned. Would you be willing to live in a house being destroyed by termites, your pet (and soon you) covered with fleas, eating moldy fruit, and facing outbreaks of dangerous insect-born diseases carried by rats, ticks, or roaches? That sounds awful too.

BE AN ENVIRONMENTAL SCIENTIST

Are you concerned about the world around you? These dedicated scientists search for ways to reduce, correct, or prevent damage to the environment. They use a mix of biology, physics, chemistry, and geology to solve the Earth's problems.

THE PASSIONATE ECOLOGIST: RACHEL CARSON

Rachel Carson was one of the very first environmental scientists. She studied biology and loved to write about science and the world around her, but she became very concerned about the impact of people on nature.

In the 1960s several big chemical companies were producing pesticides that not only killed the bugs that ate crops but the birds in the area too. In 1962 she wrote a very important book, Silent Spring, *warning of what would happen if there were no birds.*

People hadn't really stopped to think about how each species in an ecosystem depends on many others. Carson wrote: "The sprays, dusts, and aerosols are now applied almost universally to farms, gardens, forests, and homes—non-selective chemicals that have the power to kill every insect, the good and the bad, to still the song of birds and the leaping of fish in the streams—to coat the leaves with a deadly film and to linger on in soil—all this, though the intended target may be only a few weeds or insects." Is killing a weed worth it? Think about it!

THE DAMAGE WE DID

Pesticides have been around for centuries. The ancient Romans burned sulfur to shoo bugs away and sprinkled salt on weeds to kill them. In colonial times, ants were kept at bay with a mixture of honey and arsenic—a poison found in certain minerals.

In the late 1940s, chemists started mixing up toxic combinations of chemicals that were so effective that they harmed not only the targeted pest, but other creatures as well, including birds and people. Fortunately environmentalists, such as Rachel Carson, made the public aware of the dangers.

Humans have brought other miseries to the planet. Rainforests have been destroyed. Oil spills have damaged seashores. We have overfished some kinds of sea creatures, and hunters have brought dozens of animals to the verge of extinction. We must do better!

THE GOOD WE CAN DO

Many harmful chemical sprays have now been banned and more and more farmers are using natural ways to control crop damage. We have made it against the law to harm endangered species and we are fighting to stop rainforest destruction. We have become aware of how fragile our Earth is, but there is still a lot to do.

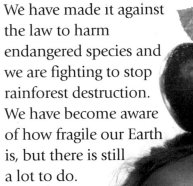

A VERY DELICATE BALANCE

Environmental scientists are hard at work trying to find new ways to protect our planet—from making sure our drinking water is safe to dealing with climate change. Conservationists are also working to protect animal habitats, conserve wetlands and woodlands, and save endangered species that are struggling to survive.

We face all sorts of challenges in the coming years. Will you be an important part in finding solutions to Earth's problems? After all, it's your planet. Don't you want it to be a nice place to live?

REVIEW AND DO

Adaptations

Structural adaptations
A body part an animal or plant HAS to help it survive.

Behavioral adaptations
Something an animal or plant DOES to help it survive.

Population

A group of the same organisms living in the same place.

Ecosystem

All the populations and nonliving things—water, rocks, and soil—that interact with one another in a certain place.

Community

A group of different populations that share an ecosystem.

Niches

The role played by a species in the community it inhabits: where it lives, what it eats, and what preys on it.

Human actions have positive and negative effects on ecosystems.

Use pages 78-79 to answer questions 1 and 2.
1. What is a structural (physical) adaptation?
2. How does a structural adaptation allow an organism to succeed in a given environment?

Use pages 80-81 to answer questions 3 and 4.
3. What is a behavioral adaptation?
4. How does a behavioral adaptation allow an organism to succeed in a given environment?

Use pages 82-83 to answer question 5.
5. Why do certain communities exist in specific habitats?

Use pages 84-85 to answer question 6.
6. For each organism listed below, describe its niche within a community.
   BLUEBERRY BUSH   **CARDINAL**   **BEAVER**   **SUNFLOWER**

Use pages 86-87 to answer question 7.
7. What are the various stages of the life cycle of a butterfly and a frog? What are the differences in how each of these organisms interacts with its surroundings at each stage of its life cycle?

Use pages 88-89 to answer question 8.
8. Create a food web using organisms from these pages that could truly exist in your region of Virginia. Be sure to label each organism as a producer, herbivore, omnivore, carnivore, or decomposer.

Use pages 90-91 to answer questions 9 and 10.
9. List one positive and one negative influence of human activity on ecosystems.
10. What is one positive action you can do to help protect an ecosystem in your community?

THINK LIKE A SCIENTIST

The Virginia state bird is the cardinal. What are its structural and behavioral adaptations? What is its niche within a community? Where would it fit on a food web?

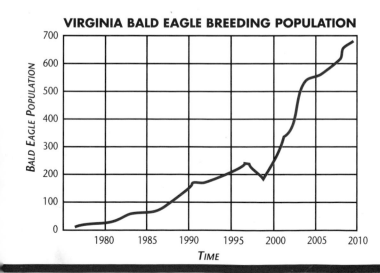

VIRGINIA BALD EAGLE BREEDING POPULATION

DATA DETECTIVE

What can you infer about Virginia's bald eagle population from 1980-2011? What impact do you think this may have on the community and habitat in which bald eagles live?

What clouds signal dangerous weather?
What causes hurricanes?
Are sleet and hail related?
Why is it so humid in the summer?

6

WILD WEATHER

OUR ATMOSPHERE

WHAT IS IT?

Think of a bird flying in the air. Now picture a fish swimming in the water. Air is to the **atmosphere** what water is to the ocean. The atmosphere is a layer of invisible gas that wraps around the planet like a blanket. Weather happens in the lower atmosphere, up to a height of about 12 kilometers. We can fly through the atmosphere in airplanes and glimpse the clouds and weather patterns below us as we gaze out the window. What causes all that weather?

ATMOSPHERE IN MOTION

Winds keep the atmosphere all stirred up. As the atmosphere above us swirls and swooshes, we feel its effects down on the ground. Every rainbow, lightning bolt, heat wave, blizzard, or tornado gets its start in the atmosphere.

Air gets pushed into large clumps, which scientists call **masses**. Some masses of air are as big as several states combined. The wind pushes those air masses around. We can often predict where those masses of air are headed, and therefore know what weather is coming our way. If we know it is raining in one location in the country, and we know which way the winds are blowing, we might expect rain ourselves.

THE LINK TO THE OCEANS

More than 70% of the Earth's surface is covered by water. As the sun shines down, the water heats up. Some of it evaporates into the atmosphere. Trees and plants add more water to the air when moisture that they pull up from the soil evaporates through their leaves and into the atmosphere. Eventually, that moisture falls down again. Next time you get caught in a downpour, remember where all that water came from. Now grab your umbrella and let's learn more.

SPEAK LIKE A SCIENTIST
· · · · · · · · · · · · · · ·
Atmosphere
(at--muss-fear)
The layer of air that surrounds the Earth.

WHAT'S UP UP THERE?

Our atmosphere is like a gigantic puffy jacket that protects us from the bitter cold of outer space. At the outermost layer of the "jacket" (closest to space) it is super-cold. The inner layers keep us warm. On a typical summer day in Virginia at sea level, the atmosphere keeps the temperature at about 26°C. If you climbed to the top of Mount Rodgers, the air temperature would drop to about 19°C. Fly higher still, to the cruising level of a jumbo jet, and the air temperature will have dropped to a frigid −45°C. Finally, at about 100 kilometers up, the atmosphere is extremely thin and the temperature is −270°C. Brrrr.

How hot is the air? How much moisture is it holding? The weather might be ever-changing around us, but the biggest reasons it rains, or snows, or is sunny happens because of these two things: the air pressure and the temperature.

KEY WORDS ABOUT THE WEATHER

Temperature
(temp-ur-a-chur)
The measure of the amount of heat energy in the atmosphere.

Front
A boundary between air masses with different temperatures and water vapor content.

Air Pressure
The pull of gravity on the atmosphere at a particular place on Earth.

Cirrus clouds
Wispy fair-weather clouds.

Cumulus clouds
Fluffy clouds that can bring storms if they grow too tall.

Stratus clouds
Smooth gray clouds that block sunlight.

Cumulo-nimbus clouds
Cumulus clouds that have grown very tall. These usually bring severe storms.

How hot or cold is it? How strong is that wind? You need the right tools to tell.

WEATHER TOOLS

What do many of us do every morning? We check the weather forecast! Will we need an umbrella? Warm gloves? Before we can learn more about the weather, let's learn about the tools used to measure it.

YESTERDAY, TODAY, TOMORROW

People who study the weather depend on special instruments to help them understand what *has* happened and to forecast what *will* happen. **Thermometers** and **anemometers** tell us about something that is happening right this very second—how hot and how windy it is. **Barometers** measure air pressure and help us predict future weather patterns. **Rain gauges** tell us about how much rain has already fallen in an area. Scientists read these tools and then input all their data into computers, which help them fine-tune their predictions.

Thermometer
(thur-<u>ma</u>-mit-ur)

This device measures the temperature of the air and tells us how hot or cold it is.

Most thermometers are long and skinny, with a bulb and thin tube filled with either red alcohol or silver mercury. Both alcohol and mercury expand when they are heated and shrink when they are cool. When the temperature rises, the expanding liquid has no place to go but up the glass tube. The liquid shrinks and lowers back down when the air temperature cools.

Round thermometers work slightly differently and are not quite as accurate, but many homeowners like the way they look.

MAKE A THERMOMETER
Go to page 103

MAKE A BAROMETER
Go to page 105

Barometer
(buh-<u>rah</u>-ma-tur)

Imagine a bathroom scale that can weigh the air around us. That's a bit like what a barometer does. It measures air pressure—the weight of the atmosphere.

Inside the case there is an airtight metal box. If the air pressure around it drops (gets lower), the box expands a little. As the box expands or contracts, a spring moves a pointer on the dial down or up. The dial has numbers and sometimes little illustrations of clouds or sun. The higher the air pressure, the drier the weather is likely to be.

Weather reporters say "the barometer is rising" when the weather will be nice. When the barometer is "falling" nasty weather often awaits.

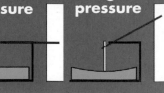

low pressure   medium pressure   high pressure

WEATHER WATCHERS

Some weather stations are on rooftops. Others, like NOAA's satellites, fly thousands of kilometers above the Earth. Sensors and cameras aboard the satellites scan the Earth and its atmosphere. They can track fast-breaking thunderstorms across America's heartland that might turn into tornadoes. With an eye on the tropical Atlantic, they can detect stormy areas, called "tropical depressions," that might evolve into hurricanes. When big forest fires burn or volcanoes erupt, weather satellites keep an eye on them as well. We depend on these "eyes in the sky," and the meteorologists who gather the data, to warn us of dangerous weather.

Anemometer
(ann-uh-mom-a-tur)

How windy is it? This device measures wind speed and direction. The most common kind of anemometer measures wind speed using three or four cups attached to a pole. As the cups catch the wind they spin. Wind speed is measured in miles or kilometers per hour, just like your car's travel speed.

The arrow with the big tail points into the wind so that you can record the direction of the wind. A "west wind" means that it is blowing from the west toward the east.

Airline pilots and boaters are especially aware of wind speed reports from areas in which they might travel. No one wants to be caught at sea in dangerous winds!

Rain Gauge

To "gauge" (gayj) means to measure. A rain gauge measures the rain that has fallen since the last measurement. Rain falls into a large cylinder, then drains through a funnel into a graduated cylinder that has measurement markings on the side.

Measurements are made in inches or millimeters. Snow gauges measure snowfall. As you know, rain, snow, and hail are all water. When there is too much rainfall we get flooding. When there is too little we call it a drought (drowt). In between is what we like best. Why do we measure precipitation? Farmers like to know if they need to give more water to their crops. People who control our drinking water supplies might ask us to use less if there has been a drought. It's always a good idea to conserve water!

MAKE A RAIN GUAGE
Go to page 109

Sometimes they look like a fluffy bunny or a ghost, but clouds are a lot more than interesting shapes.

SECRETS OF THE CLOUDS

WHAT THE CLOUDS TELL US

When you look up at the sky and all you see is endless gray, you can be pretty sure it's going to be a dull day with a good chance of rain, or snow if it is winter. Other clouds tell us a lot about the weather too. Will we have thunderstorms? Or will it be sunny?

WHAT ARE CLOUDS MADE OF?

Clouds are nothing but billions of tiny droplets of water formed around specks of dust in the air. If the air temperature is below freezing, the water crystallizes into ice. The water droplets or ice crystals are so small and light that they float, lifted gently on rising air currents.

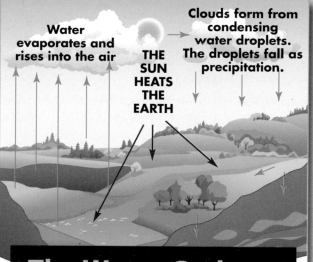

Water evaporates and rises into the air

THE SUN HEATS THE EARTH

Clouds form from condensing water droplets. The droplets fall as precipitation.

The Water Cycle

As the sun heats the Earth, water—from the ground, the oceans, and plants—evaporates into the air as water vapor. Rising air currents carry it up, where it cools and condenses as water droplets in clouds. Droplets bump into each other, get larger, and eventually fall as rain, snow, or hail to complete the cycle.

HOW DO CLOUDS FORM?

Some days the sky is cloudless—nothing but blue, blue sky. Then wisps of high, white **cirrus** clouds may show. If they continue to build, the sky may become full of clouds. That's because these three things are happening at once:

1. Water evaporates off the ocean or land, and the air becomes full of **water vapor**.

2. Rising air currents lift the water vapor to areas that are cooler.

3. As the water vapor in the air cools, it condenses into water droplets or ice crystals around tiny specks of dust. You can now see all those droplets as a cloud.

Remember, **condensation** is when a vapor cools and turns back into a liquid. Clouds are just huge clumps of condensing water vapor. Their different shapes depend on the air temperature, the humidity (how much water vapor is in the air), and how high up the cloud is.

FOUR TYPES OF CLOUDS TO KNOW

CIRRUS

Cirrus clouds are feathery. You will usually see them on fair weather days. When they thicken they may indicate approaching rain or snow.

CUMULUS

These fluffy white clouds have flat bottoms. Watch them billow out, change shape, and sometimes disappear. They usually indicate fair weather.

STRATUS

Stratus clouds are smooth and gray. They cover the whole sky and block out direct sunlight. Expect light rain, drizzle, or snow with these.

CUMULO-NIMBUS

When cumulus clouds grow really big, they get darker on the bottom and spread at the top. Cumulo-nimbus is Latin for "heap-rain," so watch out for downpours, hail, lightning, high winds, and sometimes tornadoes.

DO YOU SPEAK "CLOUD?"

Experienced sailors and pilots can often look at a cloud and tell you what the weather will be just from glancing at the sky. You can do that too. Keep a cloud journal for a month. Start by recording the time, temperature, and date. Twice a day, write a description of the clouds. What color are they? What is their position in the sky? Are they high or low, thick or wispy? Do they just hang there, unmoving, or do they float quickly by? Some cirrus clouds can travel at a speedy 160 km an hour!

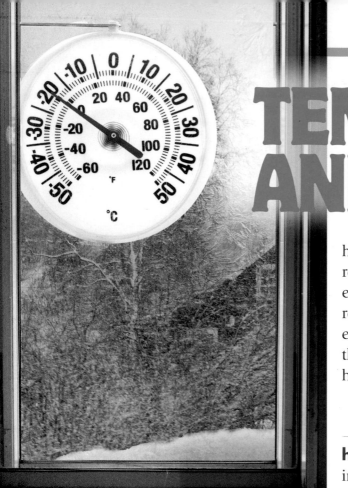

TEMPERATURE AND HUMIDITY

Air temperature is the measure of the amount of heat energy in the atmosphere. But what does that really mean? You know that the sun's rays carry heat energy to the Earth. Different parts of the atmosphere receive and hold on to different amounts of that heat energy. If there is a lot of heat energy in a certain place, the air temperature is high (or hot), if there is very little heat energy, the air temperature is low (or cold).

ICKY AND STICKY

— How hot or cold you *feel* will also depend on **humidity**, which measures the amount of water vapor in the air. When the air (at any temperature) is full of water vapor, we say it has 100% humidity. You'll probably feel pretty miserable, even if the temperature is a balmy 24°C. Why? Your sweat can't evaporate to cool you off because the air is already full of moisture. You will feel warm and sticky.

Have you ever noticed dew on grass early in the morning or fog forming in a valley or on a road? These are both due to changes in temperature and humidity. Dew and fog form when warm, moist air cools down causing water to condense. Clouds are basically just fog up in the sky. Clouds form when warm, moist air cools as it rises in the atmosphere. A lot of weather depends on the humidity and the temperature of the air.

Dew drops

TWO MEN, TWO MEASURES

There are two common scales to measure the ups and downs of temperature. Both are named after their inventors who lived in the early 1700s. The one we use in the United States is named after Daniel **Fahrenheit** (*Fah-rin-hite*), who was a Dutch glass blower—a very hot profession! Temperatures on the Fahrenheit scale have °F after the temperature number. Mr. Fahrenheit invented his scale with zero being the temperature of a salty freezing water, 32°F being the freezing point of pure water, 98.6°F being the average human body temperature, and 212°F being water's boiling point. It's a little complicated!

All scientists and people in almost every other country in the world use a scale named after Anders **Celsius** (*Sell-see-us*), a Swedish astronomer. Temperatures in Celsius have °C after the number. The Celsius scale—based on the number 10—is much simpler, with water's freezing point at 0°C and boiling point at 100°C.

TOO COLD FOR COMFORT
Temperatures below freezing can damage exposed skin, so always dress warmly if you will be outdoors for long periods of time.

MAKE A THERMOMETER
Watch the heat rise!

How does a thermometer work? Old-fashioned thermometers are thin glass tubes filled with either mercury (silver) or alcohol (usually colored red). Most of the mercury or alcohol is stored in the bulb at the bottom of the tube. The tube is sealed at the top.

As the temperature rises, the liquid in the tube expands and takes up more space. This makes the liquid rise up the thin tube. In colder temperature, the liquid contracts and its level in the tube drops.

Try it out with this homemade thermometer.

You will need:
- Tap water and rubbing alcohol
- An empty small plastic bottle with a narrow neck
- Red food coloring
- A clear plastic drinking straw
- Modeling clay

1. Pour 1/4 cup each of tap water and rubbing alcohol into the bottle. Fill about 1/8 of the bottle.
2. Add a few drops of red food coloring and swirl until mixed.
3. Put the straw in the bottle as shown, but don't let the straw touch the bottom.
4. Use the clay to seal the neck of the bottle, so the straw stays in place.
5. Cup the bottom of the bottle in your hands and watch what happens.

When you're done, pour all liquids down the drain and recycle the plastic bottle.

FROM FAHRENHEIT TO CELSIUS

If you use one scale and your friend uses the other, you are still talking about the same temperature. You can convert the numbers using some math. Here's how to convert °F into °C:

Write down the temperature in °F.	75°F
Subtract 32.	75–32 = 43
Then multiply by 5	43 x 5 = 215
Divide by 9	215 : 9 = 23.9
The answer in °C is ⟶	23.9

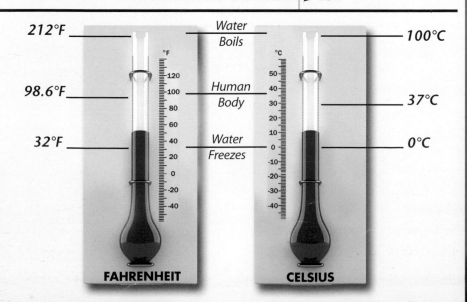

212°F	Water Boils — 100°C
98.6°F	Human Body — 37°C
32°F	Water Freezes — 0°C

FAHRENHEIT   **CELSIUS**

HOT, WARM, COLD?

Chart the temperature range in your area. Check the temperature when you wake up and when you get home from school for the next two weeks. You can check at an online weather site, watch TV, or check an outdoor thermometer. Record the highs and lows for each day along with the change in degrees between high and low. What patterns do you notice?

AIR PRESSURE

Hot air balloons fly because warm air rises above cooler air.

Wave your hands around. Feel anything? That's not just empty space you're touching. You just touched billions of pieces of air. Those pieces are called molecules *(moll-uh-kewlz)*. Air is made of molecules of different gases including molecules of water. All those molecules weigh something. The force caused by the weight of air pushing on things is called **air pressure**. You might find it hard to believe, but there are about 500 pounds of air pushing down on the top of your head right now. You don't notice it because your body is used to it.

WOOOOOOSH!

Blow up a balloon and think about what's going on in the balloon and in your lungs. Now let go of the balloon's neck. What happened? First you filled your lungs with air. Then you squeezed your lungs to push the air into the balloon. The balloon filled with air. To do this you had to increase the air pressure both in your lungs and into the balloon. When you let go of the balloon neck, the air rushed out. Why? Air flows from areas of high pressure to low pressure until the two are balanced. This is an important thing to know.

Another thing to know is that hot air takes up more space than cold air, and is therefore lighter and rises up above colder air. That's how hot air balloons can fly. But how does all this wooshing air relate to the weather?

AIR PRESSURE, WIND, AND WEATHER

Air is always moving in the atmosphere. You can see clouds flowing by. You can feel the wind blowing. Air moves because of differences in air pressure and temperature. The wind blows from areas of **high pressure** (in this case, "high" means "a lot" or "heavier" pressure) towards areas of **low pressure** (or "less" pressure). Warm air rises up and cool air sinks toward the ground. Add some water to all this air movement, and you've got lots of different kinds of weather.

High Means Dry
Areas of high pressure bring dry <u>h</u>appy weather.

Low? Oh No!
Areas of low pressure bring cloudy, wet, <u>l</u>ousy weather.

REMEMBER
Cooler air = more pressure = high pressure
Warmer air = less pressure = low pressure

WET OR DRY?

Air near the Earth's surface gets warmed up by the sun. This warm air gradually gathers moisture from oceans, lakes, and rivers, as well as from trees and other plants. Warm air can hold a lot of moisture. In areas marked **L** (for low pressure) on weather maps, the warm, humid air is rising slowly and cooling as it rises. The air's moisture then condenses as water droplets to form clouds which can bring rain or snow. In areas marked **H** (for high pressure) on weather maps, cool air is gently falling down through the atmosphere. Cool air can't hold as much moisture as hot air. This air brings clear skies because the air is so dry.

Barometers are instruments that measure air pressure. When you hear a weather reporter say, "the barometer is rising," it means that a high pressure system is on the way. The weather will be nice. If you hear "the barometer is falling," get set for precipitation, because an area of low pressure is about to surround you.

LOW PRESSURE= WET WEATHER
Bring your umbrella!

High numbers mean dry days.

HIGH PRESSURE= DRY WEATHER
Bring your sunglasses!

WET IS WONDERFUL

*Sometimes rain is a pain, but for farmers rain is a good thing. From time to time, weather patterns change and not enough rain falls. When that happens we have a **drought** (drowt). Droughts can make life difficult for many people. No rain means no crops, and that means very little food. Think about how your life would be affected if farmers could not grow their crops or feed their livestock.*

HANDS-ON SCIENCE

BUILD A SIMPLE BAROMETER

You will need:

- A plastic cup or empty can
- An 11-inch round balloon • scissors
- A rubber band • A piece of tape
- A wood skewer or long straw with the end snipped to form a pointer
- A strip of cardboard and a pen to mark readings

1. Blow up the balloon, then deflate it. This makes it easier to slip over the mouth of the cup or can. Cut off the neck and secure it with a rubber band to prevent air from seeping in.

2. Tape a long skewer to the center of the balloon as shown.

3. On a strip of cardboard, make several horizontal lines or simply mark "high and "low."

4. Note the current weather. You might check with NOAA.gov for your area's current pressure. Mark the scale where your skewer is pointing, record the date and weather outside.

Record the data from your barometer every day at the same time.

Predict what the weather might be in the next 12-14 hours.

REPORTING THE WEATHER

MAPPING AIR PRESSURE

As weather instruments gather data from both local weather stations and miles-high weather satellites, computers process that data so meteorologists can forecast weather. Which way is that hurricane moving across the Atlantic Ocean? What path might it take? How much snow will that blizzard bring? Meteorologists can also see trouble spots—the areas where high pressure is about to collide with low pressure. These areas are called **fronts** and they often bring wild weather.

FRONT LINES

Fronts are the boundaries between air masses of different temperature. There is a sharp edge between the two air masses. Most of Earth's wild weather occurs near fronts. When a cold air mass is cutting under a warm air mass and lifting it, it is called a **cold front**. The most violent weather occurs with cold fronts, because the cold air mass shoves the warm air up quickly, creating low pressure. Cold fronts often bring thunderstorms with high winds along their edge. In winter, they bring blizzards.

If a warm air mass is rising up over a cold air mass, it is a **warm front**. A warm front may cause thunderstorms, but usually it just brings lots of clouds and then light rain or snow. You often see cirrus clouds first and eventually stratus clouds or fog. Once the front has passed, the sky slowly clears, and the temperature is warmer.

A **stationary front** occurs when neither air mass is moving much at all. With a stationary front, the weather will be "stuck" for a couple of days—often with days of drizzle and rain.

WHAT'S THE WEATHER?
Weather reporters have to brave terrible conditions from time to time. You might see them standing along the shore just before a hurricane strikes, or in the middle of a blizzard. Some weather reporters are also meteorologists. Others are not.

SPEAK LIKE A SCIENTIST
·····
Front
A boundary between two different air masses that often brings big changes in the weather.

HOW TO READ A WEATHER MAP

Weather maps are packed with all sorts of useful information. Big blue Hs show high pressure systems that will bring cool, dry air and light winds. When viewed from the weather satellite, these high pressure winds spin like the hands of a clock over our hemisphere.

Low pressure systems bring a whirling mass of warm, moist air. Stormy, windy weather is often on its way. When viewed from a weather satellite, low-pressure winds spin in the opposite direction from high pressure winds in our hemisphere. Low pressure systems are represented with big red Ls.

There is a lot of important information added to a map, such as warnings of snow, possible thunderstorms, floods, and other dangerous conditions. Find Virginia on this map. What kind of pressure is it experiencing?

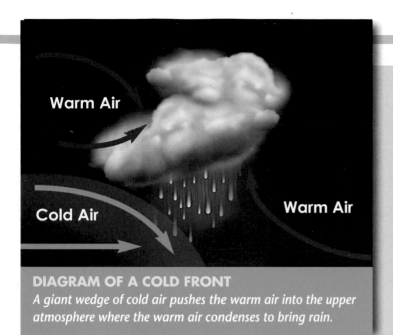

Warm Air

Cold Air

Warm Air

DIAGRAM OF A COLD FRONT
A giant wedge of cold air pushes the warm air into the upper atmosphere where the warm air condenses to bring rain.

BE A METEOROLOGIST

Meteorologists *(meet-ee-or-ol-uh-jists) are the scientists who study the atmosphere and weather. By gathering and studying data, they can often predict what the weather will be in the days to come—from high and low temperatures to how much rain or snow will fall. They issue storm and flood warnings, along with forest fire alerts. They also have special forecasts for pilots, farmers, fishing fleets, and the shipping industries. Physics, chemistry, math, and computer skills play a big part in their work.*

A Weather Map Legend

 **Stationary Front**

 **Warm Front**

 **Cold Front**

What will fall from the sky the next time a low pressure front moves in? Will it be rain? Snow? Hail the size of golf balls?

PRECIPITATION

RAIN, RAIN GO AWAY!

Remember the water cycle? The sun heats the Earth. Earth's water evaporates and rises into the much colder air. The water vapor cools, condenses, and deposits itself onto tiny floating bits of microscopic dust. Clouds fill with these water-dust drops until they can no longer hold them. But now what? Grab your umbrella! It's **precipitation**! But will it rain? Snow? Hail? A lot depends on what is happening in the atmosphere.

HOW HIGH IN THE SKY?

Different atmospheric conditions create different types of precipitation. The higher up in the atmosphere, the colder it is. That's the reason it is usually cooler in the mountains. It's the same with a cloud. Depending on how high in the cloud the moisture is, different kinds of precipitation will result. When you add in the season and temperatures on the ground, it all adds up to a variety of different kinds of precipitation falling on our heads.

RAIN OR SNOW?
The kind of precipitation that falls depends on two things: where in a cloud the water droplets gather and conditions down on the ground.

SPEAK LIKE A SCIENTIST
....
Precipitation
(pre-sip-uh-tay-shun)
Water that falls from the clouds to the Earth in the form of rain, snow, hail, or sleet.

WHAT'S THE DIFFERENCE?

RAIN When cloud droplets become too heavy to stay in the cloud, they fall toward the Earth's surface as liquid water.

HAIL These big frozen raindrops occur during severe thunderstorms. Cold air turns a raindrop into a tiny chip of ice. Violent winds push the drop back up into the cloud to be coated again and again with more layers of ice. Eventually, the hailstone is heavy enough to fall to the ground. Some hail can grow to be the size of a golf ball. Dangerous!

SLEET If a falling snowflake melts by passing through warm air, and then refreezes by passing through cold air, it becomes a tiny chunk of ice called sleet. It is easy to confuse sleet with **freezing rain**. Freezing rain starts as typical rain but freezes only after it hits the ground.

SNOW Tiny ice crystals attract each other as they fall toward the ground. Since the snowflakes do not pass through a layer of air warm enough to cause them to melt, they remain intact and reach the ground as snow.

HANDS-ON SCIENCE

BUILD A SIMPLE RAIN GAUGE

How much rain just fell?

You will need:
- An empty 2 liter plastic bottle with straight sides
- Bread knife to cut bottle (and a grown-up to help you)
- Ruler
- Waterproof tape
- Rocks or bricks

1. Ask a grown-up to help you cut an old plastic bottle in half and turn the top upside down to make a funnel.

2. Tape a small plastic ruler to the side of the bottle just past the curvy part of the base to get a more accurate measurement of the rainfall.

3. Keep the rain gauge out of direct sun. You don't want it in direct sun because the sun will speed the water's evaporation.

4. Place a few bricks or stones around the base of your gauge so it does not tip over in bad weather.

5. After the next rain, record the amount of rainfall. Empty the gauge after each measurement. Keep a log of rainfall in your area over a period of a month.

A distant boom. A blinding flash.
A howling wind. Get set for...

THUNDERSTORMS

SUPERCELLS
No, it's not a spaceship. Its a huge thunderstorm called a supercell. These storms can be several kilometers wide and deliver heavy rains, high winds, and occasional tornadoes.

A VERY SCARY SKY

The air feels moist and warm. The cumulus clouds start growing taller and taller. Their bottoms grow darker and darker. From off in the distance the first low rumbles of thunder can be heard. Soon fingers of lightning pierce the sky. What is going on?

Three things are needed to make a thunderstorm:

1. Moisture—Water in the air to form clouds and rain.

2. Unstable air—A pocket of air that is warmer than the air around it and just keeps moving up and up.

3. A lifting source—Heat from the sun is the most common cause of air being lifted. As the Earth's surface warms, the air above it heats up, and warm air always rises.

Certain types of geography can also help thunderstorms form. Mountains are air-lifters. Sea breezes can also act as triggers. And anytime a warm front and a cold front meet, conditions are perfect for a wet, wild storm.

Lightning can put on awesome displays. Each burst releases a lot of static electricity—like the shock you get from touching a doorknob, only much more massive!

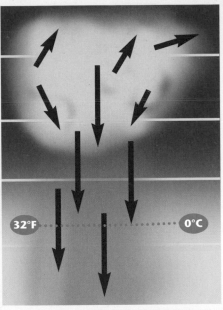

STORM PHASES

Height
40,000 ft.
12.2 km
30,000 ft.
9.1 km
20,000 ft.
6.1 km
32°F .... 0°C
10,000 ft.
3.0 km

Towering Cumulus Phase

Warm, moist air rises, cools, and condenses into a cumulus cloud. Condensation releases energy, warming the air more. Now the air inside the cloud is warmer than the air outside, making the air "unstable." The cloud grows taller. Soon it reaches an altitude where temperatures drop below freezing. Big raindrops and, often, hail form.

Mature Phase

The drops become so heavy that they fall from the cloud. It is raining now, but warm air from below is still pushing up. Things get chaotic with air moving up and down. The cloud grows higher and higher and spreads out at the top. Thunder and lightning fill the sky, and torrents of rain (and/or hail) fall to the ground.

Dissipating Phase

All that heavy precipitation stops the rise of warm air which was "fueling" the storm. With no more fuel or energy, the thunderstorm cloud dissipates (dissipate means to scatter). The only thing left behind will be giant puddles.

A WORD ABOUT WIND

Wild weather and wind go hand in hand. But what makes wind? You know that warm air rises. As it lifts, cooler air rushes in to fill the space it has left behind. Remember—nature likes things to be balanced!

If you have ever visited an ocean beach, you might have noticed a breeze. On warm days, the air over land heats up more than the air over the sea. As the "land air" rises upward, air kept cool by the water blows in to fill the space.

Now imagine the same thing happening on a much larger scale on Earth. Since the sun does not heat the planet evenly, warmer air near the equator rises, and cooler air from the polar regions flows in to replace it. Add in the spinning of the Earth and you have the wide world of wind!

The winds howl. Trees snap in half like matchsticks.
Water pours from the sky. And a giant cloud moves closer and closer...

HURRICANES

NEXT STOP, LAND
This satellite photo shows Hurricane Floyd swirling toward the Florida coast. Over 2.5 million people were ordered to leave their homes.

SPEAK LIKE A SCIENTIST
....
Hurricane
(_her_-ick-cane)
A huge, slow-moving storm that is fueled by heat and energy from warm ocean waters. Some hurricanes can be over 800 km in diameter.

DEADLY STORMS

Sometimes things go haywire in the atmosphere. A particular combination of air pressure and temperature leads to extreme weather conditions. When that happens we can end up with a scary thunderstorm, or worse—a **hurricane**. These storms can cause a lot of damage because they combine dangerously high winds with heavy rains. Trees and power lines are knocked over, roofs peel away, and streets can flood.

As the temperature rises in late spring through early fall, low pressure caused by the presence of warm, wet air creates the right conditions for a hurricane to form. This happens especially in the waters of the Atlantic Ocean off the coast of Africa.

ONE YEAR'S HURRICANES AND THEIR PATHS

Virginia

Atlantic Ocean

Off Africa

HURRICANE SEASON

The hurricane season officially begins on June 1 and ends on November 30. During that time, meteorologists anxiously study the air above the Atlantic watching for something known as a tropical depression. Trouble begins with areas of low pressure. Thunderstorms develop and warm ocean waters evaporate, rising into the clouds. If the water and air are warm enough, the winds may start to spiral, whipping themselves into a hurricane.

LANDFALL: NEW ORLEANS
Hurricane Katrina's storm surge brought terrible destruction.

BIG AND BAD

Hurricanes are huge. They can bring winds in excess of 240 km an hour. And rain! A strong hurricane can drop over two trillion gallons of water in one day. One of the scariest parts of a hurricane is called a **storm surge**, which causes huge waves to flood the coast. Every year an average of six hurricanes will strike the U.S., costing billions of dollars.

SAME STORM DIFFERENT NAME

Massive Atlantic storms are called hurricanes, but gigantic storms also form in the Pacific and Indian Oceans. If a megastorm blows across the western Pacific it is called a typhoon (*tie-foon*). The same storms in the northern Indian Ocean are called cyclones (*sy-klonz*).

And speaking of names, since 1953, hurricanes have been named after people. How would you feel about sharing your name with a hurricane?

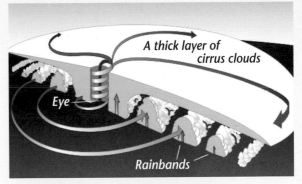

A thick layer of cirrus clouds

Eye

Rainbands

HOW A HURRICANE FORMS

If you want to make a hurricane, you need a large area of very warm ocean water (27°C or higher). As the warm water evaporates, warm, moist air will rise and condense into many monstrous thunderstorm clouds. Condensation releases heat energy, which causes more air to rise, building the storm higher. The rising air leaves behind an area of low pressure, which causes winds from all around to swirl in.

The rotation of the Earth causes the whole, huge storm to spin. It spins clockwise if it is south of the Equator, counter-clockwise if it is in the Northern Hemisphere. At first, it is called a tropical depression, then a tropical storm. When the winds blow faster than 74 miles per hour, it is called a hurricane. If the ocean stays warm, hurricanes grow stronger and stronger (They are numbered Category 1 through 5, with 5 being the worst). Winds are not the only danger. Flooding from storm surges, huge waves, and heavy rain can bring misery.

LANDFALL: VIRGINIA
In 2011, Hurricane Irene caused massive flooding and blew off roofs and home siding.

TORNADO!

These powerful storms can lift a house off its foundation!

Every year, between 800 and 1,000 **tornadoes** spin across the United States, leaving paths of debris that can be a 1.5 km wide and more than 80 km long.

Fronts are the culprits in causing tornadoes, especially in the spring when very warm, moist air moving from the east collides with hot, dry air flowing in from the west. This happens a lot in the Great Plains—the central part of the United States—which has earned the nickname "tornado alley." But even here in Virginia, tornadoes can be a real danger.

HOW DANGEROUS ARE THEY?

Winds that can carry a cow over 40 km are only part of the danger from a tornado. These scary storms also bring giant hailstones and torrents of rain. Tornadoes are born in supercells—those massive thunderstorms with cloud heights reaching more than 12 km into the atmosphere. What turns a supercell thunderstorm cloud into a tornado? Spinning winds!

A JOPLIN, MISSOURI, NIGHTMARE
Because tornadoes can form in about 15 minutes, it is difficult to warn people of the approaching danger. That makes tornadoes nature's most dangerous storm.

HOW A TORNADO FORMS

1. *Tornadoes begin when winds higher in the atmosphere are blowing faster and in a different direction than low-level winds.*

2. *The spinning is made worse by cold and warm air currents (shown here as red and blue arrows).*

3. *The spinning winds form a* **vortex** *that pulls up at the center of the storm. The spinning increases and this rotating column of air can break through the cloud and hit the ground.*

MYSTERIOUS TORNADOES

Scientists are still learning how tornadoes are created. They know that tornadoes often form in towering cumulus clouds, just like thunderstorms. When winds at two different levels above the ground blow at different speeds or in different directions, a tornado can form.

Imagine that the wind near the ground is slow and blowing from the southwest. The wind higher up is much faster and coming from the opposite direction. As they collide, it causes the air to rotate and form an invisible "tube" of air. If the storm gets enough energy from all that rising moist air, the tube can tilt and touch down on the ground. It will twist and tear up everything it touches—a bit like being in a gigantic blender.

RUN FOR COVER!

What should you do if you see a funnel-shaped cloud? Move to your basement. If you don't have a basement, move to a closet or a room away from windows on the lowest floor you have. Crawl under a sturdy piece of furniture like a dining room table. If you are outside, lie flat in a nearby ditch or hollow, away from any trees. Cover your head with your arms. Safety first!

HANDS-ON SCIENCE

TORNADO IN A JAR

See a vortex form!
You will need

- 8 oz. jar with lid
- 175 ml water
- 5 ml vinegar
- 5 ml liquid dish soap
- A pinch of glitter (optional)

1. Fill the jar with the water.

2. Add the vinegar and dish soap.

3. Sprinkle in a small amount of glitter.

4. Close the lid tightly and swirl the jar quickly, then stop. A vortex much like a tornado's will form.

As you swirl the jar around and around, the water is moved by its friction with the jar sides, but the fluid in the center has less friction, so it takes longer to start moving. At first, both the jar and the fluid spin, but as you stop swirling the jar, the fluid inside keeps spinning.

The tiny twister you are seeing occurs because the outer fluid has slowed down, but the inner fluid has not. These differences in speed of motion cause a tornado vortex to form.

REVIEW AND DO

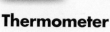

Thermometer
Air temperature

Barometer
Air Pressure

REMEMBER THESE WEATHER INSTRUMENTS

Anemometer
Wind Speed

Rain Gauge
Rainfall

REMEMBER THESE CLOUD-TYPES

Cirrus

Stratus

Cumulus

Cumulonimbus

REMEMBER THESE KINDS OF PRECIPITATION

Rain

Snow

Sleet

Hail

REMEMBER THESE AIR PRESSURE FACTS

High pressure brings fair weather.

Low pressure brings unsettled, stormy weather.

REMEMBER THESE STORM-TYPES

Thunderstorm

Tornado

Hurricane

Use pages 98-99 to answer questions 1 and 2. Copy and complete the chart below.

Instrument	Thermometer	Barometer	Anemometer	Rain Gauge
1. What does this instrument measure?				
2. How does this instrument help meteorologists?				

Use pages 100-101 to answer questions 3 and 4.

3. Use the words "water vapor," "temperature," and "condensation" to explain how clouds form.

4. What type of weather is associated with cirrus clouds? Stratus clouds? Cumulus clouds? Cumulonimbus clouds?

Use pages 102-103 to answer question 5.

5. What are the two measurement systems for calculating air temperature? Which system does the United States use? How do you think this may affect the sharing of temperature data between scientists in Europe and scientists in the United States?

Use pages 104-105 to answer question 6.

6. Describe the weather change if a barometer is holding steady at 9 AM and then begins falling at 2 PM.

Use pages 106-107 to answer questions 7 and 8.

7. What is the difference between a cold front and a warm front?

8. Draw a diagram of a cold front bumping in to a warm front.

Use pages 108-109 to answer question 9.

9. Describe the atmospheric conditions needed to create different types of precipitation including rain, sleet, snow, and hail.

Use pages 110-115 to answer question 10.

10. Thunderstorms, tornadoes, and hurricanes have one thing in common in the way they form. What is it?

THINK LIKE A SCIENTIST

A storm chaser is a person who chases severe weather. Even though many storm chasers are not meteorologists, storm chasers need a solid understanding of weather patterns. They analyze weather conditions in hopes of finding and observing severe weather. Pretend you are a storm chaser hoping to catch a glimpse of a tornado. Using the weather map on pages 106-107 and a U.S. map, where would you travel in the hope of seeing a twister?

DATA DETECTIVE

You are a meteorologist who has just been given the data in the chart below. What would you predict the weather to be on Wednesday, Jan. 4? Explain your prediction.

Date	Temperature	Barometric Pressure	Wind Speed	Cloud Cover
Monday, Jan. 2	High:44 Low:28	Rising	SW 5 mph	Cumulus
Tuesday, Jan. 3	High:30 Low:16	Falling	W 10-15 mph	Stratus

Why does the Earth move in space?

How old is the sun?

What makes the seasons change?

How did we learn about the planets?

Is the Earth still changing?

CHAPTER 7

EARTH PATTERNS, CYCLES, AND CHANGE

Both involve spinning, but they are very different!

ROTATION AND REVOLUTION

SPINNING IN SPACE

Stand still for a moment. Really still. Can you feel the Earth moving? No? Well it is! It is hard to believe, but the planet you are standing on is spinning around once every 24 hours. At the same time it is spinning, it is also traveling through space so that it makes a complete trip around the sun every 365¼ days.

There are two words that describe how the Earth moves in space: **rotation** and **revolution**. They are easy to confuse, but one is very different from the other. Stand up and spin around once. Congratulations! You just completed one rotation. Imagine a straight line going from your head to your feet. That's called an axis. You just rotated around your axis. The Earth does this too. It rotates around its axis once every 24 hours.

Now stand at the edge of the room and walk around the edge in a circle until you get back to where you started. Well done. You just completed one revolution. You "revolved" around the center of the room. The Earth does this too. It revolves around the sun, once every 365¼ days.

SPIN CYCLE
Draw an imaginary line from the top of this girl's head to her feet. That's her axis. As she spins, she is rotating around it.

PUT THE TWO TOGETHER

Now do what the Earth does: rotate at the same time as you revolve. Spin around your axis while walking around the edge of the room. Don't get too dizzy! If you really wanted to be accurate, you would have to rotate 365¼ times by the time you made one complete circle (revolution) around the room.

ROTATION: NIGHT AND DAY

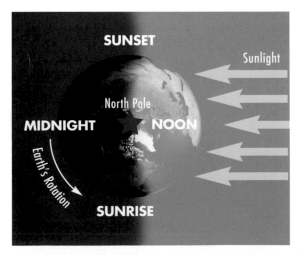

Rotation is the reason we have night and day. Day is when our particular place on the Earth is facing the sun. Night is when we are facing away from the sun. Pick a spot on the wall to look at and pretend that it is the sun. Now rotate once. You can only see that spot when you are turned toward it. As you turn away, imagine that spot "setting." As you come back around, it is "rising," like the sun.

Rotation is why people once thought the Earth was the center of the universe. Because the Earth is spinning, it appears that the sun is moving across the sky. At night it looks as if the stars are rotating around the Earth. In reality, it is the Earth's rotation that gives us this view.

MANY REVOLUTIONS

The Earth's revolution around the sun takes 365¼ days—one year. It is the time it takes for the Earth to go around the sun once and return to the same place. The other planets also revolve. The closer a planet is to the sun, the shorter its revolution and its year. Moons revolve too. While the Earth is busy revolving around the sun, our moon is revolving around the Earth about once every month.

THE SECRET OF ORBITS

Why do planets circle the sun? Gravity! If there were no gravity, Earth and the other planets would all be traveling through space in a straight line, forever and ever. But gravity *does* exist, so the planets are also being pulled by gravity toward the huge mass of the sun. The forward motion of the planet and the pull of gravity are balanced. This holds the Earth and other planets on an almost circular path and keeps them from escaping into the far reaches of deepest space.

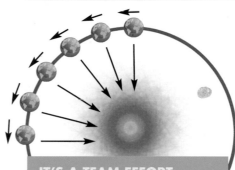

IT'S A TEAM EFFORT
Gravity pulls Earth toward the sun, but Earth also has a forward motion. Together, they make Earth's motion more of a circle.

SEEING STARS

As you learn more about the universe, look carefully at the images. Some of them are real photos and some are computer-generated artwork that looks so real that you might think they are photos. It is really important to know the difference because, although the artists base their artwork on real science, sometimes the sizes and distances of planets and stars are very different from real life. As you read, look carefully at the images in this chapter and try to determine which is a photo and which is a painting.

Is this a photo? A painting? Or a combination of both?

LINK TO THE PAST

The ancient Egyptians were pretty smart. They realized that it actually takes the Earth a little more than 365 days to complete its annual trip around the sun. What to do with that extra time? All those extra hours start to add up into days, weeks, and months!

By the time of the Ancient Roman empire, people began to depend on calendars. A Roman year was 365 days, but the extra time at the end of every year was beginning to add up. Every hundred years there was almost an additional month! Something had to be done so the emperor Julius Caesar decided to add one extra day, every four years to the calendar. Leap-day!

There are about four million people on Earth who have a leap-year birthday. Do you know anyone who was born on February 29?

Twinkle, twinkle not-so-little star.
How I wonder what you are?

This solar flare is so big, the entire Earth could easily fit inside it. Flares are giant clouds of hot solar gas.

THE SUN

SUN-DAYS

On a clear night, you can see thousands of stars in the sky. But what's the only star that looks so bright you can see it during the day? Our sun! In fact, a better name for "daylight" is "sunlight."

The reason that you can see anything at all during the day is because of light from the sun. If the sun did not exist, our planet would be a cold, dark, lifeless rock covered with frozen oceans.

The sun is about 4.6 billion years old and is the center of our solar system. All the planets (including Earth), along with other space travelers such as comets, asteroids, and meteors, revolve around the sun. As they zip along, their paths (or orbits) look like slightly squished circles known as **ellipses**.

SUN FACTS

Color: *Yellow*
Age: *About 4.6 billion years old*
Mass: *As heavy as 330,000 Earths*
Diameter: *1.4 million km through its middle*
Surface Temperature:
5500°Celsius
Core Temperature:
15 million°Celsius
What it is made of:
92.1% hydrogen, 7.8% helium, 0.1% other elements
Distance from Earth:
150 million km

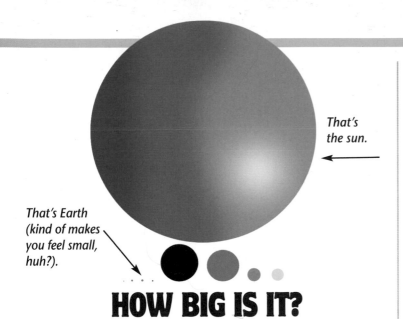

That's the sun.

That's Earth (kind of makes you feel small, huh?).

HOW BIG IS IT?

The sun is enormous! It is 99 times more massive than all of our solar system's planets (including Earth) combined! You would have to multiply the diameter (width) of Earth by 110 to get the diameter of the sun and you could fit about one million Earths inside it. But here's a surprising fact: Even though the sun is huge when compared to the planets in our solar system, it is actually just an average-sized star. Some stars are much smaller. Others are much larger.

FLAMELESS HEAT

A lot of people think the sun is on fire, but it is not burning. The sun is extremely hot and gives off light because of a process called nuclear fusion. The sun is a gigantic ball of gas made almost entirely of the elements hydrogen and helium. Its atoms zip around and crash into each other. As the sun's hydrogen atoms smash into each other, they fuse into helium. Each of these little crashes gives off light, heat, and energy. Billions of these reactions occur every second, creating sunlight.

DARK DURING THE DAY

The sun looks small to us Earthlings because it is so far away. In fact, the moon and sun seem to be about the same size in the sky. Why? Even though the sun is 400 times bigger than the moon, it happens to be 400 times farther away.

Something amazing happens when the moon travels between the sun and Earth. The moon blocks the sunlight, casting a shadow on Earth, just like when you stand in the sun and cast a shadow on the ground. The part of Earth under the moon's shadow gets almost as dark as night, even in the middle of the day! Birds stop singing, and it used to scare people. It certainly looks as if a round shadow is eating the sun! Now we understand what's happening. We call it a **solar eclipse** (*ee-klips*).

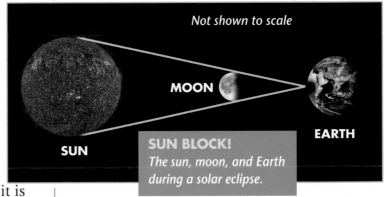

Not shown to scale

SUN **MOON** **EARTH**

SUN BLOCK!
The sun, moon, and Earth during a solar eclipse.

Every year there are several solar eclipses, but only a small section of Earth can see them. If there is a solar eclipse in your area, ask an adult how to safely view it using a hole in a piece of cardboard. Hold the cardboard above a piece of paper on the ground, and you will see a tiny image of the eclipse on that paper. NEVER, ever look directly at the sun, even during an eclipse. The light can seriously damage your eyesight.

LINK TO THE PAST

Many cultures around the world once worshipped the sun. The ancient Egyptian sun god was called "Ra." The ancient Greek sun god was "Helios." The Greeks believed that Helios drove a chariot that pulled the sun across the sky from east to west. When scientists first discovered a new gas in the sun before they ever found it on Earth, they named it helium after Helios. Helium is a very light gas, much lighter than air. We often fill balloons with helium to make them float.

THE MOON

SMASH!

Most astronomers think that a few billion years ago, when Earth was still forming, a very large object smashed into our planet and a piece broke off. This piece became our moon. The moon is about 402,000 km (250,000 miles) from Earth. If you could fly a fast jet to the moon at 1,600 km per hour, it would take you over ten days to get there. Rockets can get you there faster.

HOT, COLD, AND VERY QUIET

What is it like on the moon? The moon is a rocky, lifeless **satellite** with no atmosphere. Its surface is covered with craters—giant holes—of all sizes, from as tiny as your toe to bigger than Texas. Most of these craters are millions and even billions of years old, and were formed by meteoroids—specks of comet dust and hunks of rock or metal that fly through space at speeds ten times faster than a speeding bullet. These pelting chunks zapped into the moon's surface, and since the moon has almost no atmosphere to protect it, these space pellets left marks all across its surface.

There is no liquid water on the moon. No streams, lakes, rivers, or ponds, although scientists have discovered very small amounts of ice in small craters. The moon has no air, so there is no atmosphere to trap heat. There are no breezes. As a result, days on the moon can get hotter than boiling water, and nights are twice as cold as the coldest nights on Earth. Because the moon has no air, it is also totally silent. Soundwaves cannot travel without air. If an astronaut banged a drum on the moon, it would make no noise.

HOW BIG?
The moon is about ¼ the width of Earth.

"MOONTHS"

It takes the moon about one month (27.3 days) to revolve around (orbit) Earth. The words moon and month (think "moonth") are related. The moon rotates (spins on its axis) very slowly. Day and night on the moon are each two weeks long. Can you imagine what a two-week long day would be like?

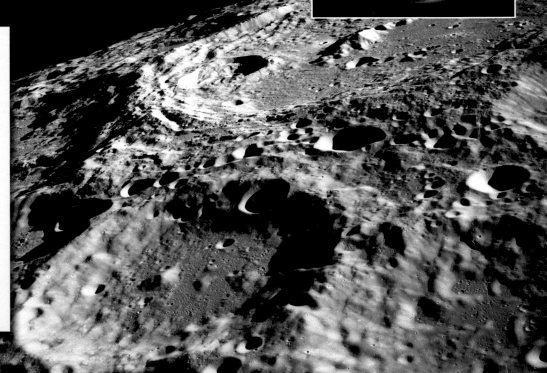

PHASES OF THE MOON

New Moon

Waning Crescent

Waxing Crescent

IN THE MOONLIGHT

Sometimes the moon looks big, round, and bright. Sometimes it is a skinny crescent. Some nights you cannot see it at all. The different appearances of the moon are called **phases**. To understand why the moon has phases, you need to understand where the sun, moon, and Earth are compared to each other. The moon shines in the sky because it is reflecting light from the sun. This is also why we have light on Earth—it's sunlight.

Half of the moon and half of Earth are always in sunlight. As the moon orbits Earth, different amounts of the sunlit parts of the moon are visible to Earth. This causes us to see different moon phases.

Last Quarter

First Quarter

Waning Gibbous

Waxing Gibbous

Waxing means we can see **more and more** of the moon. (think *wax to the max*)

Waning means we can see **less and less** of the moon.

Crescent means **less than half** of the moon is visible.

Gibbous (*gib-us*) means we can see **more than half** of the moon.

Full Moon

Remember: There is no dark side of the moon. The moon IS NOT half light and half dark!

MOON MISCONCEPTIONS

Many people think the moon has no gravity, but it does. A bullet shot straight up on the moon would still fall down. The moon's gravity is a lot smaller, so everything on the moon weighs about $\frac{1}{6}$ as much as on Earth. If you could take a scale to the moon, a 45 kg Earthling would only weigh 7.6 kg. The pull of gravity is smaller, so the scale measures less force. Another misconception is that the moon only shines at night. Surprise! It is there 24/7!

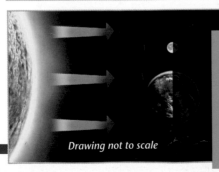

Drawing not to scale

SHINE ON
Sunlight is always lighting one half of the Earth and one half of the moon as they rotate.

THE EARTH

Eight very different planets orbit the sun. Mercury has the shortest year, Venus is the hottest, Mars has the tallest mountain, Jupiter is the largest, Saturn has the thickest rings, Uranus is the most sideways, and Neptune is the slowest. But Earth is the only planet we know of with living things—plants, fish, birds, bugs, and people. Earth is our home.

THIRD ROCK FROM THE SUN

Earth, along with Mercury, Venus, and Mars, is one of the four planets that are small, rocky, and close to the sun. The remaining four planets—Jupiter, Saturn, Uranus, and Neptune—are giant balls of gas and are much farther away from the sun. Earth is the third planet from the sun and is the only planet with just one moon. Mercury and Venus have no moons, Jupiter and Saturn have dozens of moons. But there are more reasons our planet is special.

THE ATMOSPHERE

The surface of the Earth is covered with air. We call this air the **atmosphere** and it is mostly made of the gasses nitrogen and oxygen. The Earth's atmosphere extends from the ground to distances high up in the sky. You are surrounded by atmosphere right now. Earth's atmosphere traps heat from the sun like a blanket and protects us from much of the sun's harmful rays. Without an atmosphere, Earth would be much colder at night, hotter during the day, and probably lifeless.

HOW TO BE A PLANET

Want to be a planet? You have to pass three tests. **1.** You have to be so big that your own gravity makes you round like a ball. **2.** You have to circle around a star, such as the sun. **3.** You have to have cleared your path of orbit. This means you cannot have asteroids or any other space "stuff" floating in your path. There are several "dwarf planets," including Eris and Pluto, that only passed the first two tests. They have too much space debris swirling around them to be actual planets.

EARTH FACTS

Age: *About 4.5 billion years old*
Distance from the sun: *150 million km*
Life began here: *About 3.5 billion years ago*

A WATER WORLD

If an alien ever saw a picture of Earth, its first question might be, "What's all the blue stuff?" About 70 percent of Earth is covered with water. Scientists believe that water is the key ingredient for life because so many different chemicals can dissolve in water and allow important reactions to happen. When scientists are looking for signs of life beyond Earth, they first look for evidence of liquid water.

"JUST RIGHT"

In the story of Goldilocks and the three bears, Goldilocks is always happiest when she discovers the items that belong to the baby bear because they are "just right" for her. Some scientists have called Earth the Goldilocks planet because it is "just right" for life. If Earth were closer to the sun, it would be too hot and all the water would evaporate. If Earth were farther from the sun, it would be too cold and all the water would freeze into ice. Liquid water is the key to life, and Earth has plenty of it. At 150 million kilometers away from the sun, our planet is at just the right spot for life as we know it to exist. Scientists are looking for other "Goldilocks" planets around other stars. Will they have life on them?

STANDING ON THE SUN?

What is it like on the surface of the Earth, moon, and sun?

THE SUN

You could not stand on the sun because it is a vast ball of fiery gas. It does not have a firm surface like the moon or Earth. It is extremely hot—5500°C—with a top layer that looks a lot like water bubbling and boiling in a pot. From time to time huge eruptions of gas soar upward then loop back down. These fiery ribbons of gas can be thousands of miles long.

THE MOON

Rocky, lifeless, freezing or super-hot, and totally silent. Pack a space suit because the temperature drops down to about -150°C at night. Daytime temperatures rise to above 100°C. During daylight hours it's hot enough to boil water. Darkness brings a sudden temperature drop of 250°C in just a matter of moments.

You'll have 13 Earth days of sunlight, followed by 13 days of pitch dark.

THE EARTH

Oceans, trees, mountains, meadows, deserts, ice caps, rivers, and comfy temperatures in many places make Earth a great place to hang out. The Earth has a rocky, hard surface, much of which is covered by water or soil. If you could tunnel down to the Earth's center, you'd pass through a hot liquid layer that surrounds a solid iron inner core.

Winter, Spring, Summer, Fall.
Why do the seasons change?

SEASONS

Here's a riddle. Is the Earth closer to the sun during Virginia's summer? NO! That's not the reason for the seasons. In order to understand seasons, you need to remember three things about the Earth: it is round like a ball, it is slightly tilted, and it revolves around the sun.

LET'S TALK ROUND

Shine a flashlight on a flat piece of cardboard. All the areas of the cardboard get the same amount of light. If the Earth were flat, then all parts would get the same amount of light and heat from the sun. All parts would have the same season all year round.

Now shine a flashlight on a basketball. Does the top of the ball get the same amount of light as the middle? It is the same for the Earth. Because our planet is round, different parts get different amounts of sun. This explains why the poles are cold, the equator is hot, and the parts in between have moderate temperatures. But why it is so hot in Virginia in summer and cold in winter? Read on!

LET'S TALK TILT

Imagine you could spin the Earth like a top. It would spin on its axis—the imaginary line that goes through the Earth from the North Pole to the South Pole. But unlike a toy, the Earth's axis is tilted. It leans to one side as it revolves around the sun. That **axial tilt** means that when the North Pole is tilted toward the sun, Virginia (and the rest of the Northern Hemisphere) gets more hours of sunlight and more direct sun rays, so things can really heat up. In winter, when the Earth has revolved around to the other side of the sun, the North Pole is tilted away from the sun. Daylight hours are shorter and it can get c-c-c-cold.

In spring and fall, day and night are of more equal length. The North Pole is neither tilted toward nor away from the sun, so we have mid-range temperatures.

SPEAK LIKE A SCIENTIST
·······················
Axial Tilt
(<u>ax</u>-ee-ul • tilt)

The amount the Earth is tilted in relation to the path of its orbit. Earth is tilted at 23.5 degrees.

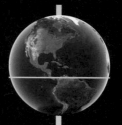 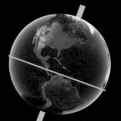

Earth if it had no axial tilt — Earth's actual axial tilt

The Earth is always tilted in the same direction!

It is **summer** in Virginia. The North Pole is tilted toward the sun. The sun is aimed at the Northern Hemisphere. We experience the "longest day" of the year. More sunlight equals more heat.

MIDNIGHT SUN AND POLAR TWILIGHT

Just how tilted is the Earth? From the middle of May until the middle of July—the time when the sun is aimed most directly at the Northern Hemisphere—the sun shines for upwards of 23 hours a day at the North Pole. But in winter, when the North Pole is tilted away from the sun, there are days when it looks like night all day long. Things are reversed at the South Pole. In our winter, when it is dark at the North Pole all day, the South Pole enjoys midnight sun. We call the darkest and lightest days the winter and summer **solstice** (<u>sole</u>-stiss).

People gather at the northernmost tip of Europe to bask in the midnight sun.

It is **spring** in Virginia. The sun is aimed at the equator. The North Pole is neither tilted toward nor away from the sun.

It is **winter** in Virginia. The North Pole is tilted away from the sun. The sun is aimed at the Southern Hemisphere. In Virginia, the sun seems to be lower on the horizon, the rays don't feel as warm, and it gets dark earlier.

It is **autumn** in Virginia. The sun is again aimed at the equator. The North Pole is neither tilted toward nor away from the sun.

THE EQUINOX

There are two more very special days each year. On those days—usually sometime around March 20 and September 20—day and night are of equal length. Once again we have the people of ancient Rome to thank for the word "**equinox**" (<u>ee-kwi-nox</u>) which means "equal night." The equinox brings us almost exactly 12 hours of daylight and 12 hours of darkness.

Blast off for a closer look at our fellow voyagers around the sun.

THE PLANETS

We may share a sun and solar system, but our seven companion-planets have little else in common with Earth. Earth is one of the four planets closest to the sun, along with Mercury, Venus, and Mars. These are called the **terrestrial** planets, meaning they have hard rocky surfaces.

The four bigger planets — Jupiter, Saturn, Uranus, and Neptune—are called **gas giants** with good reason. They are huge compared to the terrestrial planets and they are made of different combinations of gasses, mostly helium, hydrogen, and water.

OUR SOLAR SYSTEM

All the planets, their moons, and the other bits of rock and ice that orbit around the sun are parts of our solar system. There are other solar systems in the universe—other stars that are suns to a group of planets. Perhaps there is life on one of those planets, billions of miles away?

Venus

Earth

Mercury

Mars

The four terrestrial planets shown to scale.

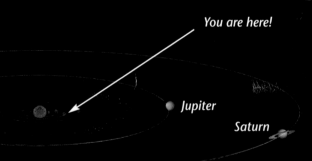

You are here!

Jupiter

Saturn

HOW FAR FROM THE SUN?
Follow the orbits of the planets. See how close the terrestrial planets are to the sun compared to the four gas giants? Can you imagine how small the sun looks from Neptune's surface?

TERRESTRIAL PLANETS

Mercury

Only slightly larger than our moon, Mercury has a very thin atmosphere. With no protection from space debris, its surface is blasted with craters. Temperatures reach 427°C during the day and then drop to -173°C at night. That's a 600 degree change!

Venus

Imagine living on a volcano. That's what the surface of Venus is like. Venus is about the same size as Earth, but it has a thick, poisonous atmosphere that traps the sun's heat making the planet so hot that metal melts on its surface.

Earth

That's us—the only planet that sustains life and the only one with liquid water. Our atmosphere protects us from the sun's harmful rays and keeps our planet's temperature "just-right" for life. The Earth's axis is tilted, creating changing seasons. We have only one moon.

Mars

The "Red Planet" is a frozen desert where nothing grows. Like Earth, Mars has changing seasons, polar ice caps, volcanoes, canyons, and weather extremes, but its atmosphere is too thin for liquid water to exist. It all evaporates. At one point very long ago, there were probably floods on Mars. Now there is only icy soil and wisps of clouds.

GAS GIANT PLANETS

Jupiter

The biggest planet has dozens of moons. Jupiter is made of the gases hydrogen and helium. If it were bigger, it would have turned into a star. Swirling clouds cover the planet. One storm, the Great Red Spot, has been raging for hundreds of years. How big is Jupiter? 1,321 Earths could fit!

Saturn

Saturn and Jupiter are made of similar chemicals. Saturn is the least dense planet. If you had a big enough bathtub, Saturn would float in it. All the gas giants have rings which are made of ice and rock, but none are as spectacular as Saturn's.

Uranus

Like the other gas giants, Uranus is mainly hydrogen and helium, but it also has a lot of methane, which gives it a pale blue tint. It is called the "sideways planet" because its axis is horizontal instead of vertical. Even though Neptune is farther from the sun, Uranus is the coldest planet.

Neptune

It is very dark and bitter cold on the last planet in our solar system. If you could float on its surface, you would be buffeted by winds reaching 1,900 km per hour. This far from the sun, it takes almost 165 Earth-years to make one revolution. Since it was discovered in 1846, only one complete Neptune year has passed.

Uranus

Neptune

When you look at Saturn's rings up close you can see that they are made up of giant frozen chunks of ice, rocks, and dust!

PUTTING THE PLANETS IN ORDER

In the cold darkness of space, the planets do not line up neatly like students getting ready to go to assembly. The planets spin in very different orbits as they circle around the sun. But it is helpful to understand what order their orbits are in, and what order they fall into in terms of their relative size.

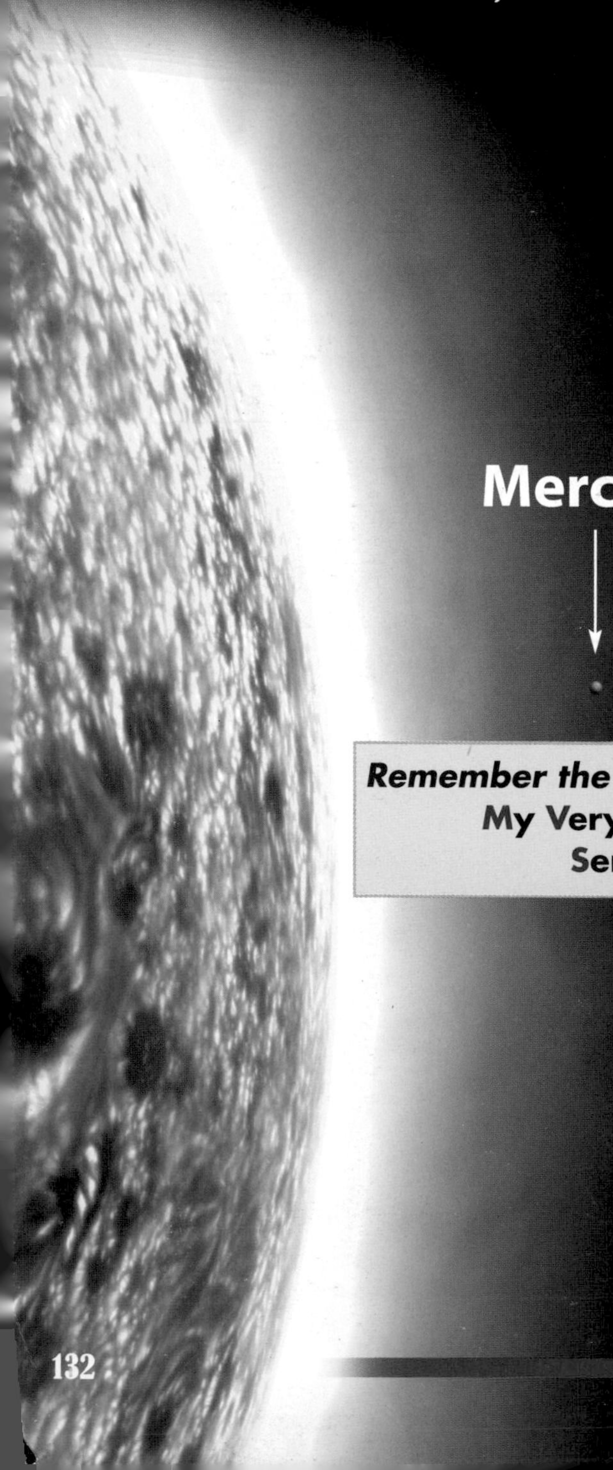

FROM CLOSE TO FAR

Tiny Mercury revolves closest to the sun and completes its orbit faster than any other planet. On faraway Neptune the sun appears as no more than a very bright star. It takes almost 165 Earth-years for Neptune to orbit the sun once.

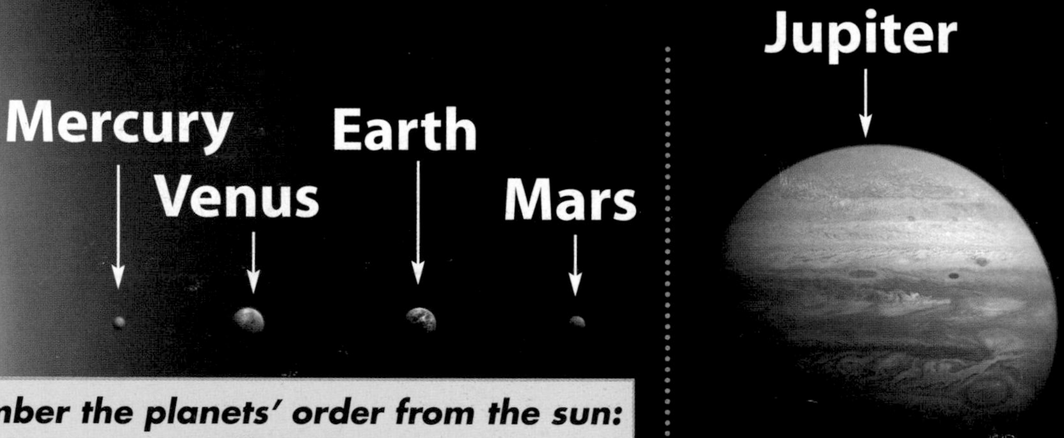

Jupiter

Mercury

Earth

Venus

Mars

Remember the planets' order from the sun:
**My Very Excellent Mama Just
Served Us Noodles**

A ROCKY DIVIDING LINE

Between the gas giants and the terrestrial planets lies an area filled with thousands and thousands of swirling rocks. These rocks are called asteroids (*as-tur-oydz*). These are all the little bits that broke off when the sun and planets first formed. For some reason, most of these space-bits have ended up in a belt between Mars and Jupiter. How big are they? Some are boulder-sized, while others are hundreds of miles wide.

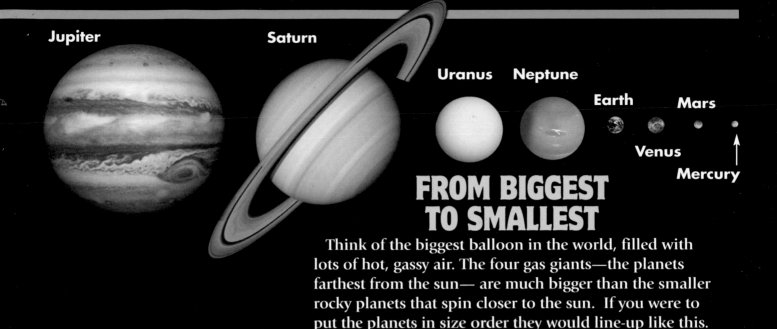

Jupiter Saturn Uranus Neptune Earth Mars Venus Mercury

FROM BIGGEST TO SMALLEST

Think of the biggest balloon in the world, filled with lots of hot, gassy air. The four gas giants—the planets farthest from the sun— are much bigger than the smaller rocky planets that spin closer to the sun. If you were to put the planets in size order they would line-up like this.

Remember the size from biggest to smallest:
Just Sing Until Noon.
Every Voice Makes Melodies!

Saturn Uranus Neptune

An artist imagines how the sun would look in daytime from the surface of Pluto.

THE DWARF PLANETS

For many years, Pluto—which orbits beyond Neptune—was called a planet. Now, it is not. What happened? In 2006, the International Astronomical Union decided that a new category was needed because they kept finding other objects that were like Pluto. We could have ended up with thousands of planets. Instead, Pluto became a "dwarf" planet along with several others. Unlike planets, dwarf planets are too small to clear debris out of their orbits.

How big are some of the asteroids? Check them out in proportion to the United States.

DISCOVERING THE SOLAR SYSTEM

A BIG ARGUMENT

Folks still argue about "what came first, the chicken or the egg?" For many hundreds of years people also argued about whether the Earth circled the sun, or the sun orbited the Earth. In fact, to even suggest that the Earth was not the center of the universe could send a person to prison in the 1500s.

We now know that Earth orbits the sun, but for centuries people did not believe this was true. The vast starry sky was filled with mysteries. All people could do was look up and decide that a particular group of stars looked like a "big dipper," or a fish, or a man with a bow and arrow. Let's meet four famous astronomers whose views on the heavens influenced people for many centuries.

"EVERYTHING REVOLVES AROUND THE EARTH"
The Influential Aristotle

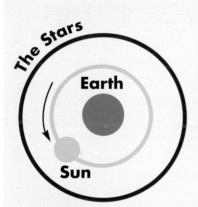

Aristotle was a great thinker in ancient Greece. He believed that the Earth stood still and that the sun, planets, and stars moved around the Earth. He wasn't alone. After all, it certainly looks like the sun moves across the sky. The moon and stars appear to do the same thing at night. Aristotle argued that if Earth was moving, we would feel it move. It also seemed logical that Earth should be the center of the solar system. For almost 2,000 years, almost everyone believed Aristotle's argument, but we have evidence now that proves him completely wrong.

384–322 BC

The Convincing Ptolemy

If you don't pay close attention to the night sky, planets look much like stars. If you watch closely though, you will notice that there are some "stars" that appear to wander through the constellations. These are not stars at all but planets. In fact, the word planet comes from an ancient Greek word that means to wander. Aristotle's Earth-centered model of the universe could not explain why the planets sometimes seemed to move backward. Ptolemy who lived in Alexandria, Egypt, believed that Aristotle was correct, but tried to improve his model. Ptolemy came up with the idea that planets moved in small circles while orbiting Earth. His model was used for over 1,000 years. However, like Aristotle, he was also wrong.

90–168 AD

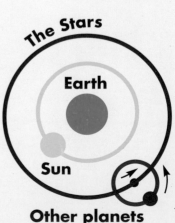

Other planets

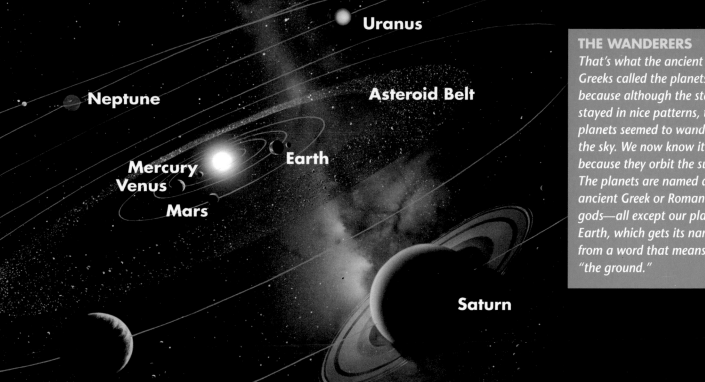

Uranus

Neptune

Asteroid Belt

Mercury
Venus

Earth

Mars

Saturn

Jupiter

© D. von Ravenswaay

"NO! THE EARTH REVOLVES AROUND THE SUN"

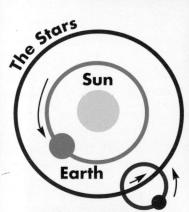

The Stars

Sun

Earth

Other planets

1473–1543

The Revolutionary Copernicus

Nicholas Copernicus is famous for being one of the first people to argue that the Earth circled the sun. This idea was considered revolutionary because It went against what everyone else thought, including the very powerful Catholic Church, which controlled what many people were taught in Europe at that time. The Copernican model of the solar system did a better job of explaining why the planets looked brighter sometimes and dimmer at other times.

The Curious Galileo

1564–1642

Although Copernicus had suggested that the Earth might move around the sun, very few people believed him. Most people still believed that everything circled the Earth. Galileo was the first scientist to use a new invention, the telescope, to study space. What he discovered shocked everyone: he saw four different moons orbiting Jupiter. This was the first real evidence that Earth was not the center of everything.

Galileo's discovery was a huge step forward in proving that Copernicus was right: the Earth (and everything else in our solar system) revolves around the sun. His discovery was so upsetting to the church-controlled government, that he was sentenced to house arrest for the rest of his life.

Galileo discovered four large moons around Jupiter.

135

What else is out there, deep in the darkest reaches of outer space?
Does the universe extend forever? How can we find out?

EXPLORING SPACE

THE SPACE RACE

In the 1950s, the two most powerful countries were the United States and the Soviet Union (which included Russia). They were bitter rivals, locked in a struggle to be the most powerful nation. It was a scary time known as the "Cold War."

One way each side tried to beat the other was with rocketry and spaceflight. In 1957 the Soviets launched the first artificial satellite ever, *Sputnik I*. One month later, they launched *Sputnik II*, which carried the first living being—a dog. Four years later, the Soviets sent the first human into space when Yuri Gagarin orbited Earth. It looked like Americans would lose the space race. But with the enthusiastic support of President John F. Kennedy, eventually Americans accomplished a tremendous goal. We sent the first humans to the moon!

ASTRODOG!
Laika, a Russian space pooch, was the first living thing in space.

THE APOLLO MISSIONS

Do you remember learning "For every action there is an equal and opposite reaction"? Scientists used that law of physics to send rockets into space.

The American space mission that sent astronauts to the moon was called the **Apollo** program. It was created by **NASA** (*National Aeronautics and Space Administration*). On July 20, 1969, during the *Apollo 11* mission, Neil Armstrong and Buzz Aldrin became the first humans to stand on the moon. As Armstrong placed one foot on the moon, he said "That's one small step for [a] man, one giant leap for mankind." It was so exciting!

The Apollo astronauts made big contributions to our understanding of the moon. They brought back moon rocks and soil samples that scientists are *still* studying, more than 40 years later. The astronauts measured solar winds and even left a set of mirrors on the moon to help with measuring and monitoring the moon's distance from Earth.

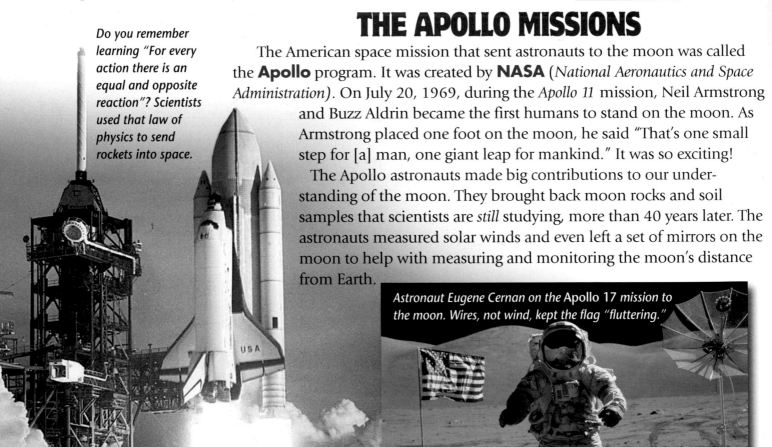

Astronaut Eugene Cernan on the Apollo 17 *mission to the moon. Wires, not wind, kept the flag "fluttering."*

The International Space Station orbits 320 km above the Earth.

THE INTERNATIONAL SPACE STATION

With the end of the Cold War, the U.S. and Russia agreed to build a space station together and to peacefully help each other explore space further. Today, scientists from many countries are doing experiments in outer space on the **International Space Station**, a large artificial satellite that orbits Earth. Scientists live and work on the space station for several months at a time. One of the things they are studying is the effect of zero gravity on our bodies. It's fun to float, but it weakens our muscles.

LOOKING FARTHER

The moon is much, much closer to Earth than the planets, sun, comets, asteroids, and other stars. Since it's hard to get to these faraway places, scientists have developed other ways of studying outer space. They use very powerful **telescopes**—instruments that make distant objects appear nearer. They can put telescopes in orbit around Earth or send them out into deeper space aboard rockets. These telescopes don't have to worry about clouds and the atmosphere getting in the way.

Some telescopes use light waves to capture images. Others use radio waves to gather information about the universe around us. Both have provided many answers to our questions about the nature of the heavens.

A Hubble telescope photo of a pair of distant galaxies. Hubble was carried into space aboard a rocket.

BEYOND OUR SOLAR SYSTEM

Our understanding of space is always changing because of new scientific discoveries. What have we learned? The Hubble telescope gave us clues that helped us estimate the age of the universe as 13.7 billion years old. Scientists believe that life might once have existed on Mars and have detected planets orbiting other stars. Could those planets have life on them? And what about enormous black holes? Black holes are a bit like cosmic vacuum cleaners that suck in energy and everything else, including light, so you can't even SEE a black hole! What would happen if you traveled into one?

Most of the universe is made of mysterious dark matter and energy, and scientists don't fully understand what those are. Every time an astronomer makes a discovery, questions are answered, but many new questions arise. Who knows what the next generation of astronomers—maybe *you*—will discover?

ASTRONOMER OR ASTRONAUT?

An **astronomer** (uh-_strah_-nuh-mer) studies outer space. How is that different than an **astronaut**? Mae Jemison, the first African American women to travel into space, was a biologist and doctor. Places like the space station need all kinds of scientists, so maybe you will work in space some day.

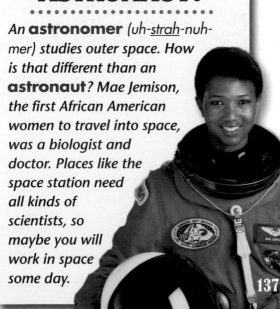

REVIEW AND DO

REMEMBER THE REASON FOR THE SEASONS
Axial Tilt

REMEMBER THE RELATIONSHIPS BETWEEN THE SUN, MOON, AND EARTH

Moon
Sun
Earth

REMEMBER THE PHASES OF THE MOON

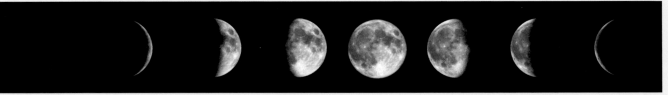

| 1. New Moon | 2. Waxing Crescent | 3. First Quarter | 4. Waxing Gibbous | 5. Full Moon | 6. Waning Gibbous | 7. Last Quarter | 8. Waning Crescent |

REMEMBER THE PLANETS

Terrestrial Planets

Mercury Venus Earth Mars

Gas Giants

Jupiter Saturn Uranus Neptune

REMEMBER THESE PEOPLE AND EVENTS

Aristotle: The sun revolved around the Earth

Ptolemy: Planets also orbited Earth

Copernicus: The Earth revolved around the sun

Galileo: Proved the Earth revolved around the sun

NASA Apollo Missions to the Moon

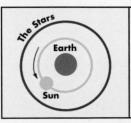

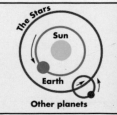

Use pages 120-121 to answer question 1.

1. Explain the difference between rotation and revolution. How long does it take Earth to complete one rotation? How long does it take Earth to complete one revolution?

Use pages 122-123 to copy and complete the chart below to answer question 2.

Approximately how big is the sun?	What color is the sun?	How old is the sun?	From what is the sun made?

Use pages 124-125 to answer questions 3-5.

3. Explain the meaning of the terms waxing, waning, and gibbous.
4. Draw and label a picture of the eight phases of the moon.
5. Why do we see different phases of the moon?

Use pages 126-127 to answer question 6.

6. Create a three circle Venn diagram to compare and contrast the surface conditions of the Earth, the moon, and the sun.

Use pages 128-129 to answer question 7.

7. How does Earth's axial tilt cause the seasons?

Use pages 130-133 to answer questions 8-10.

8. Starting with the planet closest to the sun and ending with the planet farthest from the sun, sequence the eight planets.
9. Sequence the planets from smallest to largest.
10. How are terrestrial planets different from gas giants?

Use pages 134-135 to answer questions 11 and 12.

11. How is an Earth-centered model of the solar system different from a sun-centered solar system? Which solar system model is correct?
12. Explain how Aristotle and Ptolemy's theories of the solar system were different from Copernicus and Galileo's theories.

Use pages 136-137 to answer question 13.

13. What does NASA stand for? How did the Apollo missions greatly contribute to our understanding of the moon?

THINK LIKE A SCIENTIST

Pluto was discovered in 1930 and was classified as the ninth planet in our solar system. In 2006, the International Astronomical Union created new guidelines for planets, and Pluto became a "dwarf planet." How is this an example of how our understanding of the universe changes with new information?

Planet	Revolution Time in Earth Days
Mercury	88
Venus	225
Earth	365
Mars	687
Jupiter	4,332
Saturn	10,760
Uranus	30,685
Neptune	60,189

DATA DETECTIVE

This data provides the time it takes for our solar system's planets to orbit the sun. Which two planets orbit the sun in less than one Earth year? Approximately how many Earth years does it take Mars to orbit the sun? Which two planets have the longest years?

CHAPTER 8

VIRGINIA'S NATURAL WONDERS

Virginia's Luray Caverns in the Shenandoah Valley are a series of enormous chambers. Some are ten stories high!

What is your watershed address?
How do Virginia's minerals help our nation?
What animals call Virginia home?
What will the future bring to our state?

Spectacular scenery, valuable minerals, awesome wildlife—Virginia has it all!

OUR RICH STATE

Virginia is a special place. It is a state that has a lot of everything. It is here that all our **natural resources**—trees, rocks, water, and soil—meet **human resources**—farmers, miners, fishermen, builders, and the millions of other Virginians who help make our state so great.

USING OUR NATURAL RESOURCES

Thick forests all across the state give us lumber with which to build homes and furniture, and pulp for making paper. The rich soil of the Piedmont and Valley and Ridge regions are perfect for growing fruit and raising farm animals such as turkeys, chickens, and cows. The waters that crisscross the Coastal Plain are filled with fish, clams, oysters, and delicious blue crabs. Not only does all that seafood feed us, it also nourishes the wildlife in the region. Raccoons have to eat too, you know!

Forests
Lumber to build with and pulp to make paper

Farmland
Good soil to grow crops and raise animals

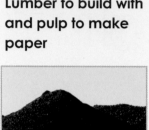

Minerals
Coal, sand, and rock for energy and building materials

Wildlife
From blue crabs to black bears, there are thousands of species

Waterways
Streams, rivers, lakes, bays, and a vast ocean

Wonders
Amazing natural formations of stunning beauty

FIVE FANTASTIC REGIONS

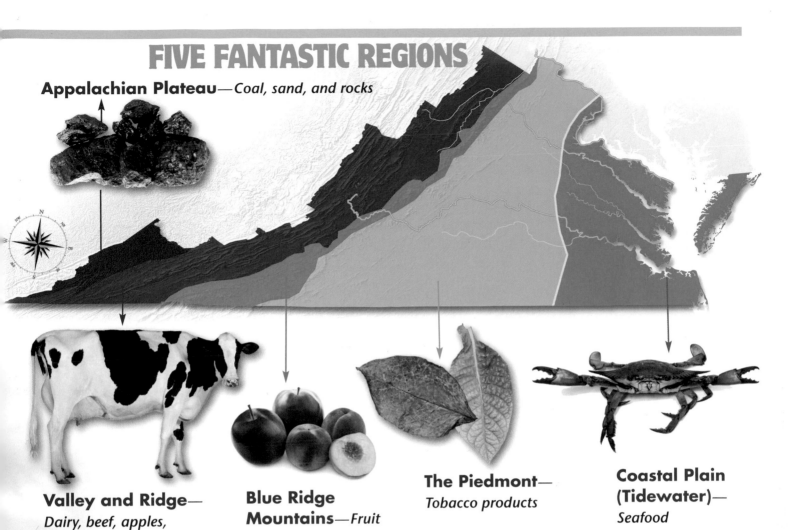

Appalachian Plateau—*Coal, sand, and rocks*

Valley and Ridge— *Dairy, beef, apples, poultry*

Blue Ridge Mountains—*Fruit*

The Piedmont— *Tobacco products*

Coastal Plain (Tidewater)— *Seafood*

NATURE-MADE, HUMAN-MADE

Even a simple rock can have great value. From deep underground we dig up coal to power factories and generate electricity. We cut slabs of granite and other stone from mountainsides and use it for construction projects. We turn sand into glass by melting it at extremely high heat. Can you imagine a world without glass?

CARING FOR OUR RESOURCES

How can we protect all these valuable resources? If we chop down all the forests or ruin the soil, if we overfish Virginia's waters or worse—poison them by using pesticides or dumping garbage—what will happen? Let's learn more about our state's valuable resources.

Turn on a tap and get a drink of water. Now think about how connected our lives are to our waters.

VIRGINIA'S WATER RESOURCES

Many homeowners drill wells to get water from aquifers.

Water is necessary for life, so think about where your drinking water comes from. Some of you drink **groundwater**. Deep underground there are holes between the soil and rocks. These pockets get filled with rain that seeps into the soil. These pockets are called **aquifers** (*ack-wuh-furz*). In some places, towns drill wells to reach an aquifer. In others, homeowners have a well and a pump to help pull the water up into their kitchens and bathrooms. If you live in a bigger town or city, you might get your water from a **reservoir** (*rez-uv-war*). These are usually large human-made "lakes" that capture water from nearby creeks and rivers and store it. Some parts of Virginia get water from rivers.

MORE THAN JUST A DRINK

Reservoirs provide drinking water, but they are also used to generate electricity. Water from **Smith Mountain Lake** is used to create hydroelectric power, while water from **Lake Anna** is used to cool the generators of a nearby nuclear power plant. These "lakes" are both human-made.

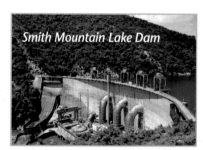

Smith Mountain Lake Dam

They were created by building dams—barriers to control the flow of water from nearby streams or rivers.

There are only two natural lakes in all of Virginia: **Lake Drummond** and **Mountain Lake**. No one is sure how Lake Drummond was formed, but some scientists think a giant meteorite created the huge crater that filled with water from the surrounding swamp. Mountain Lake may have been formed by an earthquake that shook massive rocks loose. Those rocks made a natural dam and trapped a river, keeping it from running along its course.

Rivers

Long, ribbon-like waterways that usually flow toward an ocean, lake, bay, or other river. Rivers are fed by precipitation, snowmelt, or natural springs (water from beneath the Earth's surface).

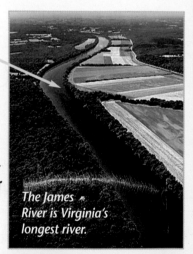

The James River is Virginia's longest river.

Bays

Large bodies of water that are surrounded by land on three sides. Bays usually have a small channel that connects them to a larger body of water, such as the ocean.

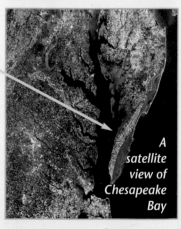

A satellite view of Chesapeake Bay

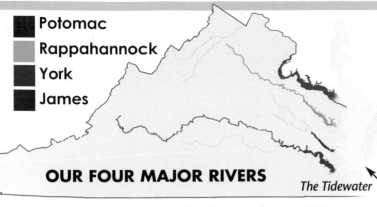

- ■ Potomac
- ■ Rappahannock
- ■ York
- ■ James

OUR FOUR MAJOR RIVERS

The Tidewater

FROM RIVER TO BAY

The Blue Ridge Mountains are the source of many of the rivers that run from higher elevations down to sea level, carrying fresh water until they are close to the ocean. Virginia's four major rivers flow into the **Chesapeake Bay**. The **James**, the **York**, the **Rappahannock**, and the **Potomac** rivers have helped shape our state. They provided drinking water, fish and shellfish to eat, and an easy way to travel in the days before roads or cars existed.

Lake Drummond is in the Great Dismal Swamp, in southeastern Virginia.

Lakes

Large inland bodies of water. Almost all lakes hold fresh water and are fed and drained by small rivers or streams.

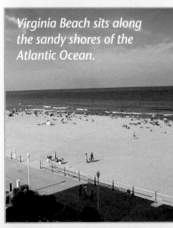

Virginia Beach sits along the sandy shores of the Atlantic Ocean.

Oceans

Mammoth bodies of salt water. There are five of them. Oceans cover more than 70% of the Earth's surface and contain 97% of the planet's water.

FROM BAY TO OCEAN

The Chesapeake Bay flows into the **Atlantic Ocean** at Hampton Roads, which is also called the Tidewater area. Here the daily rise and fall of the tides affect the lives of so many people! These are some of the most productive waters in America—brimming with blue crabs, oysters, clams, and lots of different, delicious fish.

Every year about 500 million tons of seafood are harvested from the Tidewater, which feeds not only our state but are exported to feed our nation and some parts of the world.

A FUN PLACE TO PLAY TOO
Besides giving us drinking water, a power source, a food source, and a means of transportation, Virginia's waters can be tons of fun to play in!

THE CHESAPEAKE WATERSHED

It covers parts of six states. Over 3,600 species depend on it to survive. Now let's explore it.

Let's pretend your school just held a car wash. What happens to that soapy water? Some of it might seep into the ground. Some of it might drip into a storm drain. But then what happens? It will begin to soak down into underground streams, where gravity will pull it to even lower levels. The soil may clean some of it, but in many parts of Virginia, some of that soapy water will eventually wash into the Chesapeake Bay **watershed**.

Should car washes be banned? No! Just choose soaps without phosphates. If you can, park cars on grass and wash them there. Soil helps to filter wastewater.

SIX STATES LINKED TOGETHER

The Chesapeake Bay watershed covers parts of six states and Washington, D.C. Over 16 million people share the watershed, so if someone in Pennsylvania dumps toxic chemicals into a river or stream, it can affect millions of people living hundreds of miles away.

Think about that. Fertilizers from a farm in New York can end up in the Chesapeake Bay! A pesticide sprayed on a field of lettuce in Maryland could end up flowing into our waters. Everything we do—washing our dogs, watering our lawns, flushing our toilets, driving our cars, and even turning on the lights—has an impact on the creeks, streams, and rivers that lead to the bay.

THE BIGGEST ESTUARY IN AMERICA

*An **estuary** (_ess-chu-err-ee_) is a place where salt water from the ocean mixes with freshwater from rivers and streams. The Chesapeake watershed is the largest estuary in the United States. Estuaries are important to the ecosystem because their brackish waters (another name for a mix of salt and fresh water) provide habitats for a wide range of plants and animal species such as shrimp, oysters, and crabs.*

SPEAK LIKE A
SCIENTIST
····················
Tributaries
(trib-you-terr-eez)
Streams that feed larger
streams, lakes, or rivers.

These blue lines show Virginia's major rivers and streams. There are about 150, along with thousands of other small creeks that crisscross the state.

Find the rivers nearest to where you live.

WE ALL LIVE DOWNSTREAM

Even if you live in the Blue Ridge Mountains or in an apartment building in a big city, you still live in a watershed. The Chesapeake Bay watershed covers about half of Virginia. The rest of our state's waters flow into two other major drainage areas. If you live in southwest Virginia, then your water will flow into the Gulf of Mexico through the Mississippi River. If you live in Virginia's southern edge, your water flows into North Carolina's Outer Banks. But no matter where you live, everything you do affects a watershed.

CARING FOR THE WATERSHED

Because the Chesapeake watershed is so big it is of enormous importance to the health of our state and nation. Learn as much as you can about the bay. Find out what animals live there and how they survive. Adopt a species—such as the blue crab or osprey—and learn all you can about it. And the next time you give your dog a soapy bath outside, learn how to do it in a bay-friendly way. The health of the watershed is the job of everyone.

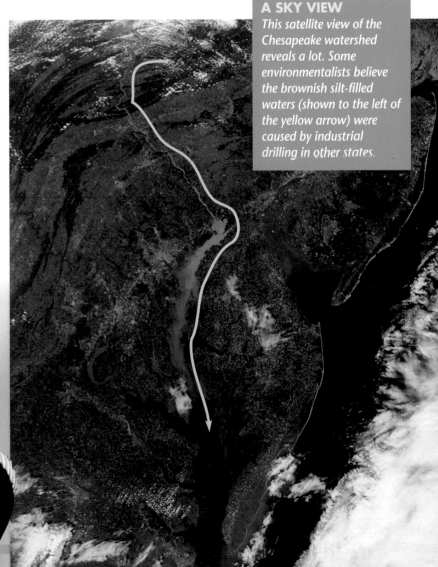

A SKY VIEW
This satellite view of the Chesapeake watershed reveals a lot. Some environmentalists believe the brownish silt-filled waters (shown to the left of the yellow arrow) were caused by industrial drilling in other states.

YOUR WATERSHED ADDRESS

You have a street address and a school address. Let's learn about another important address.

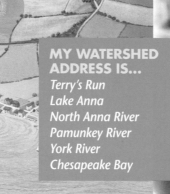

MY WATERSHED ADDRESS IS...
Terry's Run
Lake Anna
North Anna River
Pamunkey River
York River
Chesapeake Bay

WHAT DOES A WATERSHED LOOK LIKE?

Look carefully at this illustration of a watershed area. Snowmelt in the mountains forms streams that feed into rivers. Some small rivers create lakes, while others merge with other small rivers to form wider, bigger rivers that flow into bays and, eventually, the ocean. Virginia's four major rivers, the Potomac, Rappahannock, York, and James, all flow into the Chesapeake Bay and finally the Atlantic Ocean. By following the way waterways link together, you can find your watershed address.

WHAT'S YOUR WATERSHED ADDRESS?

1. Find the nearest creek, stream, or river to your home. The name of the closest body of water is the first part of your watershed address. Write it down.

2. Where does the water flow next? Trace the creek to the next body of water on a map. That's the next part of your address.

3. Keep following the water-trail on a map until you get to a major river, then a large bay, and finally the Atlantic Ocean or the Gulf of Mexico. That's the last part of your watershed address.

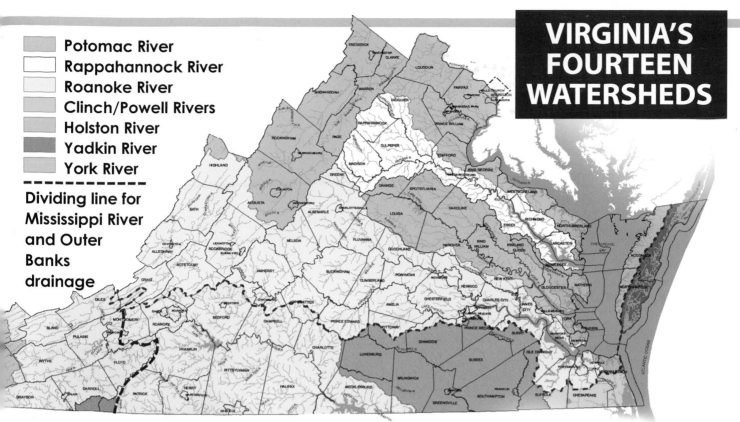

Potomac River
Rappahannock River
Roanoke River
Clinch/Powell Rivers
Holston River
Yadkin River
York River
- - - - - - - - - - -
Dividing line for Mississippi River and Outer Banks drainage

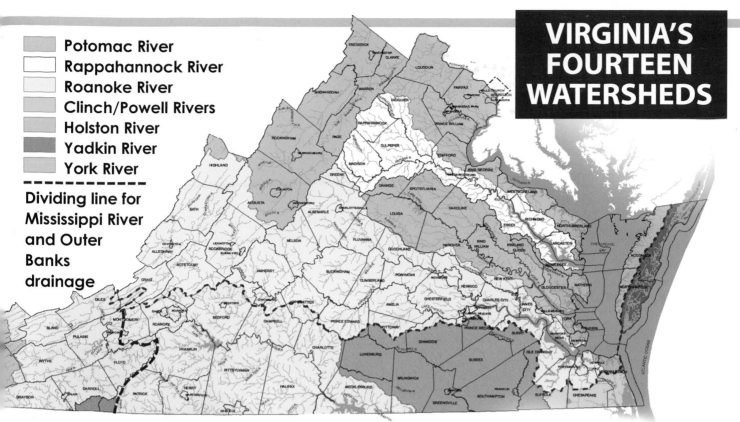

VIRGINIA'S FOURTEEN WATERSHEDS

Did You Know?

Virginia's New River is the oldest river in North America and second only to the Nile River in Africa as the oldest river in the world.

DIVIDING VIRGINIA'S WATERS

Our state has a lot of creeks, streams, rivers, lakes, and bays. Using the state's rivers as a guide, Virginia has been divided into 14 different mini-watersheds that feed into the three major watersheds—the Chesapeake watershed, waters that drain to the Gulf of Mexico, and the Outer Banks. Which mini-watershed do you live in? Brush your teeth, take a bath, do the dishes. Your unused water will flow into one of these places.

HANDS-ON SCIENCE

GO WITH THE FLOW

Two ways to see a watershed in action

1. Ask a grown-up to lend you a brownie or cake pan. Crumple pieces of scrap paper to make "mountains" at one end of the pan. In the middle, make some "hills." Lay clean paper at the opposite end from the mountains to represent the bay and ocean. Using water-based magic markers, color the edges and ridges of your mountains and hills. Then drip water on the mountains. What happened?

2. You'll need two cake pans this time. Foil brownie pans work well too. Place a large brick or rock in one pan. Place a chunk of sod (a square of grass with soil attached) in the other. Pour equal amounts of water on both. What happened?

That excess water that did not soak into the soil is called "runoff." Runoff occurs in areas where there is a lot of concrete, paving, and other hard surfaces. Everything that drips onto pavement, from dog pee to motor oil, will end up in the watershed. Find out how you can safely dispose of hazardous household waste in your area.

DON'T POLLUTE DRAINS TO WATERWAYS

149

The tissue you use for a runny nose, the pages of this book, the box that holds your morning cereal—they all depend on the trees and forests.

VIRGINIA'S TREES, PLANTS, AND SOIL

Let's stop for a minute and say "thank you" to the trees. Virginia's forests are like lungs for our state because trees filter pollution and produce oxygen. They also anchor the soil, help balance the climate, and protect the watershed. Without trees we would suffer greatly!

GREEN RESOURCES

Every part of our state is linked to forests and the industries they support. What are some of the things that can be made with timber? Telephone poles, boat docks, houses, plywood (a material made of layers of pressed wood chips), furniture, flooring, shipping crates, and pulp and paper products—from cardboard to toilet paper.

Some Virginia counties manufacture wood and paper products. Others grow or maintain forestlands. Over 65% of our state has woodlands used for industry, and more than 140,000 people in Virginia work in a business related to our forests.

Some of our forests grew naturally. Others were planted by people. We call these planted forests **cultivated** (_cull-te-vay-tid_) **forests**, and they are very important. Managing forests responsibly by cutting and replanting is good for the environment. Over the past years, our state has planted more than 250 million new trees! That's a lot of timber!

A TALL PINE
Loblolly pines grow up to 100 feet tall. They are the most important commercial timber tree in Virginia. Many birds, such as bald eagles and osprey, call these trees "home."

WHY CUT TREES DOWN?

Trees are living things, but they do not live forever. Just like people, they grow old, and they can get sick. Sick trees are more easily attacked by harmful insects and can also get diseases that may spread to other trees. And as trees die, they can become fuel for destructive forest fires. If it is done carefully, it is actually a good thing to harvest timber.

LINK TO THE PAST

When settlers from England arrived in Jamestown in 1607, the trees of Virginia helped save them. Wood products became the first cash crop for the struggling colony. One of the first manufactured products sent back to England was lumber, used for shipbuilding. Another wood product was resin—a sticky sap used to seal boats to prevent leaking. And soon, tobacco plants would save the colony.

A tree nursery is a place where new forests begin.

The American cranberry bush grows in Virginia's boggy areas. Its red berries are a favorite of local birds.

WOOD AND WATER

Did you know that forests help protect our watersheds? Trees and forest soils hold large amounts of rain, reducing the runoff—tons and tons of dirt—that can pollute streams and rivers. This helps a watershed absorb more clean rainfall. Forests help reduce flooding and erosion. Trees also protect water quality by trapping pollution and absorbing it into their leaves like a giant set of sponges.

PLANTS TO CHERISH

Trees are just one part of Virginia's "green world." Our state also has a great variety of other plant resources—more than 3,500 different species. That's quite a bouquet!

Native plants are well-suited to the growing conditions of Virginia and are in better harmony with the soil. For the animals of our state, native plants offer a familiar and healthier source of food. Most native plant species do not even need extra watering, fertilizers, or pesticides because they are such a good fit. This helps the watershed by reducing harmful runoff. When colonists from Europe arrived in the 1600s, they brought many plants with them that were not native to the area. These plants, which are sometimes called exotic plants, do not have the same benefits as native plants. They can create problems by taking over land where native plants usually grow.

THANKS, SOIL

You cannot have mighty trees and lush plants without good soil. All that rich dirt underfoot helps give our state fertile farmlands on which to grow vital crops that are the foundation of our economy. The soil nourishes our woodlands and the forests that provide a home for all sorts of wonderful critters. Virginia even has an official state soil, known as *Pamunkey soil.*

MORE THAN JUST WOOD

Our forests, flowers, and soil are a vital natural resource—protectors of our environment and "home sweet home" for birds, insects, and animals. Virginia's soil and land also provide lots of great recreational opportunities. Why not visit one of Virginia's 19 state forests? You can hike, camp, peek at the wildlife, do some bird-watching, fish, hop on a horse, and enjoy the leafy splendor of Virginia's most precious natural resources. Take some time to enjoy them!

LIVING CREATURES

This young opossum will grow to be about the size of a small house cat.

What do big-eared bats, black vultures, northern pine snakes, bobcats, and slippery oysters have in common? The are all native Virginians!

LIVING RESOURCES

The woodlands and waterways of our state shelter many thousands of native species. Some slither along the weathered rocks of the Blue Ridge Mountains. Some are furry foragers, munching on handfuls of ripe summer berries in the Valley and Ridge. Some, like the fierce and solitary mountain lion, are best left alone. And some, like the Shenandoah salamander, can *only* be found in Virginia. Some species are thriving. Others struggle to survive. Sadly, a few are headed for extinction. Let's learn more about where and how they live—right here in Virginia.

Shenandoah salamander

ON THE LAND

Virginia has animals both large and small. Black bears are the largest mammal in our state. They start out as tiny half-pound cubs (a human baby weighs about seven or eight pounds at birth), and can grow up to become 150-to-500 pound adults. Black bears are very shy and do not like to be around people, but they DO like to be around food, so always take care when you are camping in an area with bears.

Virginia white-tail deer are a common sight in much of the state. The underside of their tails has a bright white patch that makes it easy for their young ones to follow as they dart through dense woodlands. Virginia is also home to coyotes, bobcats, beavers, foxes, skunks, woodchucks, and the very rarely seen mountain lion.

CREEPY CRAWLERS

When the first settlers arrived from England in 1607, they quickly found some unwanted company—mosquitoes! Virginia's warm, moist summers are a perfect climate for all sorts of creeping, buzzing, flying, biting insects. Horseflies make picnics a misery. Ticks can burrow into flesh and bring diseases.

Of course all bugs are not bad. Virginia's bees pollinate crops and are tasty food for birds and many mammals. The creepily-named Assassin bugs (which turn other bugs to mush with a special toxin) and ladybugs are like nature's bug spray. They eat other insects and help to keep the bug populations under control.

And let's not forget the hugely important decomposers such as earthworms, that help break down fallen trees and leaves. We need them!

SNOUT TO SNOUT
Never get between a mother bear and its cub. These moms are very protective.

A raccoon

AMPHIBIANS AND REPTILES

Amphibians (*am-fib-ee-inz*) are cold-blooded animals, including frogs, toads, and salamanders. If you live near a pond, perhaps you have heard screechy croaking sounds in the evening? That's a chorus of male frogs calling out to find mates. Virginia has 27 native species of frogs and toads.

Salamanders look like lizards and have an amazing ability: they can regrow lost limbs! Virginia has 55 different kinds of salamander, and they can usually be found taking shelter in the moist soil under rocks.

Let's not forget the **reptiles** —turtles, lizards, and snakes. There are three snakes you should be aware of: the northern copperhead (found all over the state), the eastern cottonmouth (be careful if you live in Virginia Beach!), and the timber rattlesnake that lives in the Blue Ridge Mountain, Valley and Ridge, the Appalachian Plateau, and western Piedmont regions. These snakes are all venomous and quite dangerous. Never poke a snake!

A Timber Rattlesnake

STATE CRITTERS

Did you know that Virginia has an official state bird, insect, and mammal to represent it?

STATE INSECT
Tiger swallowtail butterfly

STATE BIRD
Cardinal

STATE MAMMAL
The Virginia big-eared bat

IN THE AIR

There are all sorts of amazing birds perched in Virginia's trees. Eagles and other birds of prey, such as owls and hawks, are always on the lookout for a tasty meal—perhaps a few field mice or even a fresh skunk. Vultures prefer their food dead. These scavengers can often be found pecking away at roadkill. Gulls and osprey of the Coastal Plain prefer freshly plucked fish or shellfish. Rare red-cockaded woodpeckers create homes for other species, especially bees and wasps, as they peck away at the tall pines of Virginia's forests. Think about how these animal communities work, right here in our forests, seacoast, and fields. All of these animals need one another, and we need them.

153

Deep beneath the surface, in the mines of Virginia, human meets rock. This is the story of how we use our state's minerals to better our lives.

OUR ROCKY RESOURCES

Coal, limestone, granite, sand, and gravel—just a pile of rocks? Think again! Without them we would have no windows, no schools, no paved roads, and we would freeze in the winter!

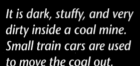

It is dark, stuffy, and very dirty inside a coal mine. Small train cars are used to move the coal out.

FIVE ROCKS TO REMEMBER

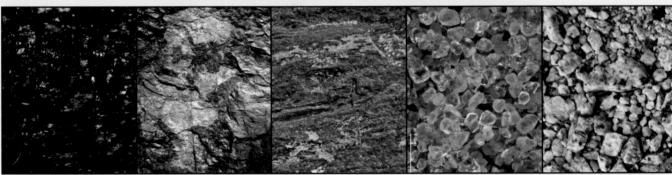

Coal
The number one fossil fuel used for energy in Virginia. It is a hard rock made of ancient pressed plant material that burns easily.

Limestone
Crushed, it is used for the construction of asphalt roads. It is also ground up to make cement.

Granite
A very hard, strong, long-lasting stone that is used for buildings, floors, monuments, and kitchen countertops.

Sand
When melted at very high heat, quartz sand turns into a liquid that is then used in making glass, ceramics, and in construction.

Gravel
An assortment of different rocks that have been broken down into very small pieces. Gravel is used in driveways and road construction.

MINING IN VIRGINA

How do we get all these valuable minerals? It's not easy! They must be dug from a **mine** or cut from a **quarry**. Mines are a series of tunnels dug deep beneath the ground. At one time, gold and silver were mined in Virginia.

A WORD TO KNOW

Quarry
(kwa-ree)
A large, solid rock area from which stone is cut away.

WHAT IS COAL?

Coal, a fossil fuel, is made from swamp plants that lived around 300 million years ago. Back when dinosaurs roamed the Earth, plants were enormous. Their big leaves stored lots of the sun's energy. When the plants died, they sank into the swamps and formed peat bogs. Lots and lots of layers of dead plants built up and, as the Earth changed, rivers and seas covered them with layers of sand and soil. Over millions of years, the intense heat and pressure from the weight of everything on top squeezed out all the water and eventually pressed the peat into coal. Coal is sometimes called "buried sunshine." Burning coal releases the energy that has been stored for millions of years.

DIGGING COAL

Almost all of Virginia's coal can be found in the Appalachian Plateau. Coal is Virginia's most valuable mineral resource, but getting it out of the ground

A mountaintop strip mine in nearby West Virginia

is not easy. There is a saying in the coalfields: "All the easy coal is gone." Huge amounts of rock and soil have to be removed to get to the coal. One of the ways to do this is with **strip-mining**. Since the coal is inside a mountain, the mountain has to be dug away. A hot topic these days is mountaintop removal. Trees are cut down and the entire mountaintop is blasted away. The leftover rock and debris are pushed into nearby valleys where they interrupt the flow of streams and hurt the watershed.

USING COAL

Half the coal produced each year in Virginia is used for generating electricity. The coal is burned to heat water, which creates steam that spins turbines that turn generators to make electricity. Scientists are busy working on new ways to get coal to burn more cleanly. Some think "clean coal" may be a future energy source that will curb air pollution and control climate change.

CUT, CRUSHED, AND MELTED ROCKS

There are other valuable minerals and rocks in Virginia. **Limestone** and **granite** are two types of rock that are very valuable to us. They are used in the construction business in slab form and, along with **gravel**, in roadways all across the state in crushed form. Crushed limestone is an important part of concrete, used to build bridges, dams, and home foundations.

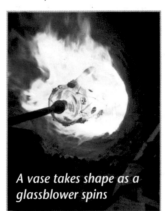

A vase takes shape as a glassblower spins

Look at all the glass around you. Where would we be without windows? Most glass is made by melting a type of **sand** that comes from a mineral called quartz. You need tremendous heat to melt rock—temperatures of 1,400 to 2,000°C, depending on the sand. If you are making a drinking glass or bowl, the molten glass is then spun as it cools and formed into shapes. Luckily we have a lot of quartz sand in Virginia!

Cutting limestone at Virginia Tech.

HOKIE STONE

Virginia Tech, one of Virginia's most famous universities, has something very special. It has a unique limestone called Hokie Stone. Five-foot-thick, boulder-sized stones are cut from a 40-acre quarry owned by the school. These huge slabs are then cut into smaller blocks. Almost all the buildings at the school are built using these gray, black, tan, and pink colored blocks.

When you are a grown-up what will Virginia be like?

OUR FUTURE

Everything changes. It is the nature of the world in which we live. Some changes bring a better quality of life. Others are harmful to our planet. The one thing you can be sure of is that change will come to Virginia.

Some changes will happen because of global warming. Others will occur because of growing numbers of people flocking to the state. As towns and cities grow bigger, it impacts our forests and strains our resources. This in turn impacts all the creatures that depend on their chosen habitats for food and shelter.

HUMANS VS. NATURE

People have had the biggest impact on the environment. Early settlers in Virginia cleared trees to plant tobacco and other crops. Growing towns and cities led to more habitat destruction. Overhunting and deforestation led some species, like the passenger pigeon, to completely die out. Other animals, such as wolves and panthers, have been forced to move elsewhere.

Settlers from Europe brought new species that were not native to American soil. New breeds of dandelions sprouted, honeybees buzzed, and brown trout swam in "new world" rivers, sometimes crowding out native species. We overfished and overhunted. We built dams to control our rivers and then built factories alongside them that dumped garbage and dangerous chemicals into once-clean waters.

WHOSE BACKYARD IS IT?
Deer have been forced to find food in neighborhood backyards, due to the destruction of their habitat in many areas.

CASE STUDY: VIRGINIA'S OYSTERS

Oysters may look slimy, but they are amazing creatures. Each oyster is a little water-treatment plant that helps to clean the Chesapeake Bay. As an oyster takes in water, it removes the nutrients through a gill system. This filtering process removes phytoplankton and other small organisms that grow in the water and use up oxygen. For hundreds of years oysters thrived in Virginia, and the Chesapeake Bay looked quite different than it does today. It was crystal clear down to a depth of twenty feet.

By the early 1900s the oysters were in serious trouble. They were overharvested for food and had also been ripped from their reefs by machines and then ground up to be used for poultry feed, in fertilizer, and for road construction. As the oyster reefs that kept the bay healthy were destroyed, it had an impact on the water quality of the bay itself. With fewer oysters filtering the waters, the bay soon became cloudy and starved for oxygen. How do you think that impacted all the other species that live in or near the bay?

For the last few years there has been a big effort to rebuild the oyster reefs. In 2010 more than 76 million oysters were added to the Chesapeake Bay in the hopes of improving the water quality. Caring for the bay will help!

ROOM FOR IMPROVEMENT

Today people have become aware of the dangers of pollution and the need for conservation. Some of the most polluting factories have been shut down. The government has established an environmental program, called Superfund, to clean up toxic waste dumps. From time to time, fishing has been banned to allow fish populations to increase.

Species that are in danger of extinction are being protected. Forests are being replanted and land trusts are preserving wilderness for future generations. Remember these words from Captain John Smith, the man who helped save the Jamestown colony back in 1608. He said, "Heaven and Earth never agreed to frame a better place for man's habitation than Virginia." Let's keep it that way.

MORE THAN JUST SHADE
Plant a tree. Trees not only provide wildlife habitats, they also help cut down on erosion which helps keep muddy run-off out of our drinking water. Trees also remove carbon dioxide from our air.

WHAT CAN YOU DO?

You may be a kid, but you can play a big role in making our state cleaner and "greener." The things you do in your community have a big impact. You've heard it before, now hear it again! Reduce, reuse, recycle! And pitch in right now to make Virginia a great place to live in future years.

1. Adopt a Stream
The Virginia Department of Conservation and Recreation has a program that allows you to be the guardian of a small stretch of a nearby stream.

2. Plant a Garden
The Virginia Department of Environmental Quality invites you to start a garden. They also offer information about natural ways to control insects instead of using harmful pesticides.

3. Save the Bay
Conserve water, start a compost pile, and reduce your use of electricity. That will mean less sewage treatment and pollution from power plants.

Together we can keep Virginia an awesome place in which to live!

REVIEW AND DO

REMEMBER THESE VIRGINIA WATER RESOURCES

Ground-water | Lake | River | Reservoir | Bay | Atlantic Ocean

REMEMBER THESE WATERSHED FACTS

A watershed is an area over which surface water—and the materials it carries—flows to a single collection place

"We all live downstream"

REMEMBER VIRGINIA'S MINERAL RESOURCES

Coal | Limestone | Granite | Sand | Gravel

REMEMBER OUR FORESTS

Natural

Cultivated

REMEMBER VIRGINIA'S LAND AND SOIL USES

Fishing

Farming

Mining

Use pages 142-143 to answer questions 1 and 2.
1. What is the difference between a natural resource and a human-made resource?
2. What are six natural resources found in Virginia?

Use pages 144-145 to answer question 3.
3. Copy and complete the chart below.

VIRGINIA'S WATER RESOURCES	What are the characteristics of this water resource?	What is an example of this water resource in Virginia?
RIVERS		
LAKES		
BAYS		

Use pages 146-149 to answer questions 4 and 5.
4. Explain the meaning of the statement, "We all live downstream."
5. What is a watershed address? How do people determine their watershed address?

Use pages 150-151 to answer questions 6-8.
6. Explain how a cultivated forest is different from a natural forest.
7. How are natural and cultivated forests important resources in Virginia?
8. How does Virginia's soil help support a variety of life?

Use pages 152-153 to answer question 9.
9. Choose a Virginia animal, insect, amphibian, or bird and explain why Virginia's environment is well-suited for that creature.

Use pages 154-155 to answer questions 10 and 11.
10. What are five of Virginia's most important mineral resources?
11. Why are mineral resources important?

Use pages 156-157 to answer question 12.
12. Other than the three suggestions listed on page 157, what are two things you can do to help protect and improve Virginia's resources?

THINK LIKE A SCIENTIST

The Virginia Watershed Alliance would like to add a slogan to go with the statement, "We all live downstream." Use your science reasoning to write the next part of the slogan for everyone to understand how their actions impact Virginia's water resources. You might even make a poster.

DATA DETECTIVE

Look at the map of Virginia on page 143. What can you infer from the map about some of the types of careers and jobs available to people in each region?

GLOSSARY

Adaptations: Physical characteristics and behaviors that allow plants and animals to satisfy life's needs and respond to the environment.

Air mass: A very large volume of air often hundreds of miles wide and several miles high that maintains consistent temperature and humidity as it travels across the surface of the Earth.

Air pressure: The pull of gravity on the atmosphere at a particular place on Earth. High pressure systems bring cool, dry air and light winds. Low pressure systems bring warm, moist air often followed by stormy, windy weather.

Air temperature: A measure of the amount of heat energy in the atmosphere.

Aquifers: Pockets or holes deep underground that are filled with water that has seeped into the soil.

Asteroid belt: The thousands of rocks that broke off when the sun and planets first formed and now orbit the sun in a region of outer space between the orbits of Mars and Jupiter. Some asteroids are boulder sized, while others are hundreds of miles wide.

Astronaut: A person trained for spaceflight who participates in a space mission and conducts research inside and outside the spacecraft or space station.

Astronomer: A scientist who studies the solar system and the universe beyond.

Atoms: The smallest units of matter that exist either singly as elements or in combinations that form a new substance.

Axial tilt: The amount the Earth is tilted in relation to the path of its orbit.

Bar graph: A graph that uses horizontal or vertical rectangular bars to compare amounts in a side-by-side format.

Barometer: A device that measures air pressure and helps meteorologists predict future weather patterns.

Bay: A large body of water that is surrounded by land on three sides. Some bays have a small channel that connects them to a larger body of water, such as an ocean.

Behavioral adaptations: The types of activities organisms perform which help them meet a life need. Some are learned from parents or other members of the same species, like hunting skills.

Camouflage: A structural adaptation that lets an animal blend into an environment so that the animal becomes almost impossible to see.

Carnivores: Creatures that eat mostly meat.

Celsius: An internationally accepted scale used to measure temperature.

Chemical properties: The way a substance may change or react to form another substance. For example, some metals rust when exposed to air. Paper burns when it meets a lit match.

Circuit: The pathway on which an electric current travels. A circuit is an unbroken link between a power supply, such as a battery, and object waiting to be powered, such as a lightbulb.

Cirrus clouds: Wispy, white fair-weather clouds. When they thicken they may indicate approaching rain or snow.

Closed circuit: A circuit with a complete pathway so electricity can be delivered.

Community: All the different populations of plants and animals that live together in the same place.

Conclusion: A final answer to an original question or hypothesis based on all the information gathered during an experiment.

Condensation: Formed when a gas cools and changes back into a liquid. Clouds are visible masses of condensing water vapor.

Conductors: Materials that allow electrical currents to pass more easily.

Constants: Things that remain the same on purpose during an experiment.

Control: The object or group of objects in an experiment that are not changed by the independent variable.

Crescent: The phase where less than half of the moon is visible.

Cultivated forests: Acres of trees planted and managed by people who cut and replant as needed to provide a renewable source of timber.

Cumulonimbus clouds: Cumulus clouds that have grown very tall and are darker on the bottom and spread out at the top. They usually bring severe storms.

Cumulus clouds: Fluffy white clouds with flat bottoms that billow out, change shape, and sometimes disappear. They usually indicate fair weather.

Current: The flow of electricity.

Decomposers: Organisms that help enrich soil by breaking down the remains of dead and decaying plants and animals.

Dependent variable: Something in an experiment that can be measured or observed to see how it responds to a change made to an independent variable.

Dormancy: A period when life functions are slowed or temporarily suspended because of seasonal changes in the environment.

Dry cell: A container full of chemicals that react with one another to become a source of electrons. Every dry cell has a positive and negative end. When you link the two ends with a wire, electrons are able to flow in a circuit. Often called a battery.

Dwarf planet: A spherical object orbiting the sun that is similar to a planet but not large enough to clear its orbit of other objects.

Ecosystem: All the populations of living and nonliving things—water, rocks, and soil—that interact with one another in a certain place.

Electricity: A form of energy made by electrons. There are two kinds of electrical energy: current electricity and static electricity.

Electromagnet: A magnet created by the flow of electric current through wire wrapped around an iron rod. Unlike permanent magnets, electro-magnets can be turned on and off and made more powerful or weaker.

Electrons: Parts of an atom with a negative charge that circle around the outside of the nucleus.

Embryo: The start of a seed. When pollen reaches the ovules of a plant, it fuses into an embryo that will develop into a seed.

Energy: The ability to do work.

Estuary: A place were salt water from the ocean mixes with freshwater from rivers and streams and provides a unique habitat for a wide range of plant and animal species. The Chesapeake Bay watershed it the largest estuary in the United States.

Ferns: Plants with feather-like fronds and no flowers or seeds. They reproduce by releasing spores.

Food web: A diagram that links organisms to all their varied food sources in a community and shows the flow of energy. Each sequence of what eats what is known as a food chain, and each food chain starts with the sun.

Force: Any push or pull that causes an object to move, stop, or change speed or direction.

Friction: Resistance to motion created by two objects moving against each other. Friction makes heat.

Fronds: The feathery leaves of ferns.

Front: A boundary between air masses with different temperatures and water vapor content that often brings big changes in the weather.

Gas giants: The four largest planets: Jupiter, Saturn, Uranus, and Neptune. All are made of different combinations of gasses, mostly helium, hydrogen, and water.

Gibbous: The phase where more than half of the moon is visible.

Graphs: Numerical or descriptive information sorted into a quickly understood visual format. Bar graphs compare amounts in a side-by-side format. Line graphs show changes over time. Picture graphs use symbols to compare amounts in a side-by-side format.

Gravity: A pulling force between objects. The more massive the object, the stronger the pull.

Habitat: The environment or home of an organism..

Herbivores: Organisms that eat only plants. These include small and large mammals, insects, and sea creatures.

Human resources: The people and their skills that are used to produce and provide goods and services in an economy.

Humidity: A measure of the amount of water vapor in the air.

Hurricane: A huge, slow-moving storm that is fueled by heat and energy from warm ocean waters and combines dangerously high winds with heavy rains.

Hypothesis: An explanation based on scientific reasoning that can be tested to see if it is correct. A hypothesis usually includes an "If _____, then_____."

Independent variable: Something changed by the experimenter on purpose to see how it affects the outcome.

Inertia: An object's resistance to changes in its speed or direction.

Inference: A conclusion based on evidence about what has already occurred.

Instinct: Behavior an animal is born with and does not need to be taught.

Insulators: Materials that reduce or prevent the flow of electricity.

Kilogram: A metric system unit used to measure mass.

Kinetic energy: The energy of motion. Objects in motion are releasing kinetic energy.

Lake: A large inland body of water. Almost all lakes hold fresh water and are fed and drained by small rivers or streams.

Laws of motion: The laws that govern the action and reaction of physical objects with respect to motion, force, and speed.

Life cycle: The changes that occur from birth through becoming an adult.

Line graphs: A graph that uses lines to show changes over a period of time.

Liter: A metric system unit used to measure volume.

Magnetic field: The area reached by a magnet's positive and negative forces.

Magnetism: A force that can attract or repel certain substances. The rules of magnetism are that opposite poles attract and like poles repel.

Mass: A measure of the amount of matter in an object.

Matter: Anything that has mass and takes up space.

Mechanical energy: Electrical energy associated with motion. It powers appliances that have moving parts.

Meteorologist: A scientist who studies the atmosphere and weather and often can predict future conditions.

Meter: A metric system unit used to measure dimensions and distance.

Metric system: A way of measuring dimensions, distance, mass, and volume used by scientists around the world, and based on the number 10.

Migration: Moving from one region to another and then back again to avoid difficult weather, to find more food, or to raise babies more safely.

Mimicry: A structural adaptation that lets certain species look like other more dangerous ones.

Mine: A series of tunnels dug deep in the Earth from which minerals like coal are extracted.

Mineral resources: Substances that come from the Earth that are either metallic, like gold, silver, and copper, or nonmetallic, like granite, limestone, and sand.

Moon phases: The different appearances of the moon as it orbits the Earth.

Mosses: Small furry-looking plants that grow in close clumps in damp, shady locations. They do not have seeds or flowers, but reproduce using spores.

Motion: A change in the direction, position, or speed of an object.

Natural resources: Things found in nature that can be used by people to satisfy life's needs. Earth's natural resources include air and water, plants and animals, soil and rocks, and fossil fuels.

Neutron: A particle in the nucleus of an atom that has no charge.

Niche: The role played by a species in the community it inhabits: where it lives, what it eats, what preys on it, what it does, and what it needs.

Observation: The basis for forming a hypothesis based on something you see, feel, hear, taste, smell, or touch.

Oceans: Immense bodies of salt water. There are five of them. Oceans cover more than 70% of the Earth's surface and contain 97% of the planet's water.

Omnivores: Organisms that eat both plants and animals. Omnivores range in size from large mammals to small birds. Most humans are omnivores.

Open circuit: A circuit with a broken pathway so electricity cannot be delivered.

Orbit: The path an object makes as it revolves around another object.

Organism: Any living thing on the planet

Parallel circuit: A circuit with two or more pathways for the electricity to flow upon. If one is blocked, electricity can still flow.

Permanent magnet: A magnet that creates and retains its own magnetic field without the need of an electric current.

Pesticide: A chemical used to kill insects and other pests that are destructive or harmful to plants and animals.

Photosynthesis: The process by which a plant uses sunlight to convert carbon dioxide and water into sugar to use as a food source.

Physical properties: Characteristics that can be observed and used to describe objects. Shape, material, size, and color are some examples.

Physicist: A scientists who studies all the different forces at work in the world.

Physics: The science that studies energy and the way objects move and react.

Picture graph: A graph that uses symbols to compare amounts in a side-by-side format.

Pistil: The stalk in the center of a flowering plant down which the pollen travels.

Pollen: A tiny grain-like substance that starts the process of seed-making in many plants.

Pollination: The process by which pollen is transferred to the sigma of the same or another flower. Pollen enables fertilization of plant embryos that will develop into seeds.

Population: A group of organisms of the same kind living in the same place. A school of fish, a herd of cattle, and a flock of geese are all examples of a population.

Potential energy: Energy that is stored. To be used, potential energy must be converted into kinetic energy. Examples include a roller coaster at the very top of the track and an arrow about to be released.

Precipitation: Water that falls from the clouds to the Earth in the form of rain, snow, hail, or sleet. The kind of precipitation that falls depends on two things: where in a cloud the water droplets gather and temperature on the ground.

Prediction: An educated guess about what you expect to happen in the future based on past experience and careful observation.

Producers: Plants that make their own food and provide energy to animal species.

Proton: A particle in the nucleus of an atom that has a positive charge.

Qualitative data: Descriptions of what can be observed, such as relative size, color, shape, smell, or other properties. It does not rely on measuring tools.

Quantitative data: Descriptions using number measurements such as width, height, volume, speed, or temperature.

Quarry: A large area of solid rock from which stone is either cut away in blocks that are used for construction or is crushed for use in concrete and other building materials.

Radiant energy: Energy associated with light. Sunlight is a major source of radiant energy. Lightbulbs and X-rays are examples of radiant energy created by electricity.

Rain gauge: A device that measures how much rain has fallen since the last measurement. Measurements are made in millimeters.

Reservoir: A large man-made lake where water is collected and stored.

Resistor: Something, such as a wire within a lightbulb, that slows the flow of electrons, allowing only some to pass.

Revolution: A circular journey by one object around another.

Rivers: Long, ribbon-like waterways that usually flow toward an ocean, lake, bay, or other river. Rivers are fed by precipitation, snowmelt, or water from beneath the Earth's surface.

Rotation: The spinning of a sphere around an axis.

Satellite: Something that orbits another object of a larger size.

Scientific method: A systematic approach to learning about the world by identifying a question or problem; developing a hypothesis and designing an experiment to test it; and then carefully observing, recording, and analyzing the results.

Seed: One way plants reproduce. A seed is a developed embryo that—with the right soil, warmth, and water—can grow into a new plant with all the characteristics of the parent plant.

Sepal: The part under the petals that protects the flower as it develops.

Series circuit: A circuit in which electricity has only one path on which to flow but which can power multiple objects.

Simple circuit: A single circuit with one power source for one object and one switch.

Solar eclipse: When the moon travels between the sun and Earth, it blocks the sunlight and casts a shadow on Earth.

Solar system: All the planets, their moons, and the other bits of rock and ice that orbit the sun.

Speed: How fast and how far an object moves in a certain amount of time.

Spore: A microscopic one-celled organism from which certain plants, including ferns and mosses, reproduce. Unlike a seed that needs to be pollinated to grow, a spore has everything it needs to reproduce and can grow into an exact copy of itself.

Stamen: The parts of a flowering plant that surround the pistil. They are covered with pollen.

Static electricity: The discharge of electricity into the atmosphere. Lightning is an example.

Stigma: The sticky tip at the top of the pistil that receives the pollen.

Stratus clouds: Smooth gray clouds that cover the whole sky and block out direct sunlight. They often produce light rain, drizzle, or snow.

Structural adaptation: A physical characteristic developed over many generations that helps a living thing survive more easily in its habitat, such as fur, webbed feet, or thumbs.

Switch: A device to open or close a circuit. In the on position, the circuit is complete, or closed. A switch to the off position breaks the circuit and makes an open circuit so electricity cannot be delivered.

Terrestrial planets: The four planets with hard rocky surfaces that are closest to the sun: Mercury, Venus, Earth, and Mars.

Thermal energy: Energy associated with heat. When electricity passes through wire loops made of certain kinds of metal, the flow of electrons is slowed. This creates friction, which makes heat.

Thermometer: A device that measures the temperature of the air and tells us how hot or cold it is.

Tornado: A dangerous funnel-shaped column of air that reaches from a thundercloud down to the ground. It has spinning winds that can exceed 400 km per hour.

Tributary: A streams that feeds a larger stream, lake, or river.

Vapor: A substance such as smoke or fog that is suspended in the air.

Variable: Something in an experiment that can be changed and that could affect the outcome.

Vortex: A mass of spinning fluid or air.

Waning: The phase of the moon where it appears to be shrinking because less and less of it is visible each night.

Watershed address: A watershed address begins with the closest body of water (creek, stream, or river) to your home, followed by the next body of water it links to. This linking process continues until the water-trail reaches a major river, a large bay, and finally, for a Virginia watershed address, the Atlantic Ocean or the Gulf of Mexico.

Watershed: An area of land where all the water above and below ground flows to the same place.

Waxing: The phase of the moon where it appears to be growing larger because more and more of it is visible each night.

CONVERSION CHARTS

Length

1 centimeter (cm) = 10 millimeters (mm)

1 meter (m) =100 centimeters (cm)

1 kilometer (km) = 1000 meters (m)

1 inch = 2.54 centimeters (cm)

1 foot = 0.30 meters (m)

1 meter (m) = 3.28 feet

1 kilometer (km) = 0.6 miles

1 mile = 1.6 kilometers (km)

Speed

1 mile per hour (mph) = 1.6 kilometers per hour

1 kilometer per hour = 0.62 miles per hour

Volume

1 liter (l) = 1000 milliliters (ml)

1 fluid ounce = 29.6 milliliters (ml)

1 liter (l) = 33.8 fluid ounces

1 gallon = 3.8 liters

Mass

1 milligram (mg) = 0.001 grams (g)

1 gram (g) = 0.001 kilograms (kg)

1 kilogram (kg) = 1000 grams

1 gram (g) = 0.035 ounces

1 ounce = 28.35 grams (g)

1 pound (lb) = 0.45 kilograms (kg)

1 kilogram (kg) = 2.2 pounds (lb)

1 ton = 2000 pounds

1 metric ton = 1000 kilograms (kg)

Temperature

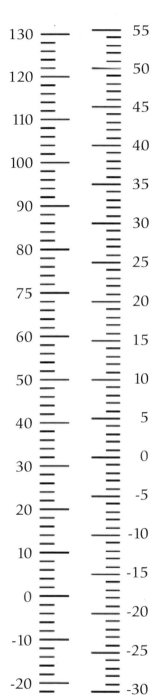

INDEX

PICTURE CREDITS

Bye-bye for now.

SEE YOU NEXT YEAR!

More exciting science awaits.